THE DAWN OF TIME

BY
ROBERT J. FOLEY

ILLUSTRATED
BY
GEORGE BALBAR

THE HAUNTED PRESS

ISBN: 1-895528-05-4

Foley, Robert J. 1941-
Canada's Story Book One
The Dawn of Time
by Robert J. Foley
Includes index

Illustrated by:
Balbar, George 1930-

The Haunted Press,
A Division of 314340 Ontario Limited
4219 Briarwood Avenue,
Niagara Falls, Ontario
L2E 6Z1

Canadian Cataloguing in Publication Data

Foley, Robert J., 1941-
    Canada's Story

Includes index
Contents: Bk. 1. The Dawn of Time
ISBN 1-895528-05-4

1.Canada - History. I Balbar, George. II. Title.

FC164.F64 1997   971.   C97-932381-9
F1026.F64 1997

Dedicated
to
the
memory
of
my nephew
Jim Foley
1973-1996

He dreamed the dreams of
Samuel de Champlain and Étienne Brûlé
and longed to see what was around the next bend in the river.

CONTENTS

PREFACE

In the past books written on the history of North America have assumed that time began with the arrival of the European explorers. The truth is that civilizations flourished on this continent long before the Vikings first looked west across the northern sea in 990 C.E.. The first Homo Sapiens to settle in the "New World" some 27,000 years ago lived, loved and struggled to survive in the wilderness much as our ancestors did 400 years ago.

This book attempts to tell, not so much the history, but, the story of Canada. Although the facts are historically correct, I do not consider myself to be an historian, either by formal education or avocation. I am a storyteller with a passion for the history of my country, a history, by the way, that is as exciting as that of any country on this planet.

This is book one in the series and it tells Canada's Story from the dawn of time to the destruction of the Hurons in 1649. It is intended to show the contribution of all the peoples who have settled this land from the First Nations to the French explorers who risked everything that we might have a country today that we proudly call Canada.

I would like to acknowledge the contribution to this series of St. Catharines illustrator, George Balbar. His original drawing, so meticulously researched, helps bring Canada's Story to life.

Robert J Foley
Niagara Falls, Ontario
October 12, 1997

THE DAWN OF TIME

Be fruitful, and multiply, and replenish the earth, and subdue it: and have dominion over the fish of the sea, and the birds of the air, and over every living thing that moveth upon the earth. - The Book of Genesis

Canada's story begins in the distant past of prehistory before the age of the dinosaurs in the Paleozoic Era, which began with the Cambrian Period some 600 million years ago and ended 230 million years ago. The theory put forward is that during this time and during the Carboniferous and most of the Permian periods North America, Europe and Asia formed a supercontinent called Laurasia. Australia, India, Southern Africa, and South America formed another supercontinent called Gondwana. In this period, between 230 and 345 million years ago, Laurasia's climate was temperate and was widely forested supporting a large variety of amphibians and early insects. In the late Carboniferous period the first reptiles appeared. The great forests were made up of scale trees, tree ferns, and giant horsetails. These materials are excavated and mined today as coal.

The Mesozoic Era began 230 million years ago with the Trias Period in which the great reptiles continued to evolve. In the Jurassic Period the dinosaurs appeared and continued into the Cretaceous Period. The evidence of dinosaur populations has been found throughout Canada, especially in the west. It is during this time that the supercontinents began to break up and Laurasia broke into two major bodies, North America and Eurasia.

It is during this period that the long reign of the reptiles and dinosaurs came to an end. The extinction of these giants who roamed the Canadian landscape ended the Mezozoic Era some 63 million years ago. The present era, the Cenozoic, ushered in the age of the birds and mammals, setting the stage for the coming of humans into the equation. It is during this time that the Rocky Mountains were formed as the great pressures of the continental movement lifted this great spine from the Yukon to South America.

Homo Sapiens, however, did not evolve in North America and the continent was ruled by prehistoric animals such as the wooly mammoth and the musk ox until fairly recently. The climate of the north was also much different from today. Fifty million years ago the Arctic Islands were forest covered. Tropical and subtropical plants grew in abundance in southern Canada and the northern United States. Beginning 12 million years ago a definite cooling trend began and the plant life of Canada changed dramatically.

One hundred thousand years ago the last great ice age descended on northern Europe and Canada. Glaciers formed spreading great ice sheets more than a kilometre deep across the landscape.

How were these massive ice sheets able to form and cover such a vast area of land? At the beginning of the last ice age large amounts of snow fell in central Labrador, Keewatin (Northwest Territories) and along the Rocky Mountains. The summer sun was not warm enough to melt the snow that accumulated over successive winters. Each winter the precipitation added to the mass of snow and ice. Over the summers the snow melted through the lower levels forming ice and creating a glacier. The weight of the accumulated snow gradually distorted the ice below and the pressure caused the glaciers to move. The glaciers crept forward, dragging along the rock, sand and clay, held fast in their icy grip. The glacier became an irresistible force that cut its way through the countryside, leveling hills and gouging out valleys.

Three ice sheets covered Canada during the last ice age. The Labrador Glacier, centered in Labrador, spread over the Maritimes, Newfoundland, Quebec, and parts of Ontario; the Keewatin Glacier had its centre in the Northwest Territories, it covered parts of Ontario, Manitoba, Saskatchewan, Alberta, the Northwest Territories, and the Yukon. These two joined on a line that ran north and south through the centre of Hudson's Bay to form the Laurentide Ice Sheet. It reached as far south as New England, and covered much of the states of Ohio, Indiana and Illinois. In the west its penetration south of the border was minimal reaching down into northern portions of the Western United States. The Cordilleran Ice Sheet covered British Columbia, the Rocky Mountains and the western edge of Alberta.

1

**Hunting
the
woolly
mammoth.**

The ice sheets ebbed and flowed as climate conditions changed. Great herds of prehistoric animals followed the edge of the ice in search of grazing land. Giant bison and mastodons competed with woolly mammoths and giant ground sloths for food. These in turn were hunted by predators like the saber tooth tiger, the American lion and the short faced bear. About 30,000 years ago the stage was set for the coming of the greatest predator of them all; man.

Two things made the introduction of humans to North America possible. One of the phenomenons that accompanied the spread of the ice sheets was a drop in the level of the seas. Sea levels are thought to have dropped as much as 100 metres during the height of the Ice Age. The other factor has to do with the amount of precipitation that fell. Siberia, Alaska and parts of the Yukon remained ice free because of the relatively small amounts of snow that fell each winter. This, combined with the lower sea levels, formed an

ice free land bridge estimated to be 1,500 kilometres wide, called Beringia, which joined Siberia and Alaska.

The people who lived in Siberia were hunters and gatherers who followed the herds of mastodons and mammoths, which supplied them with food, clothing and shelter. Their weapons of the hunt were spears tipped with stone points. Each day the hunters would fan out in search of game. The skill of the hunter and the availability of game spelled the difference between survival and death.

The young hunter leaned over the small fire warming himself, for though it was spring, the cold Siberian winds could still search out the gaps in his fur parka and leggings. His stomach complained of the scarcity of game in the vicinity and he worried about the fifty or so men, women and children in his band. Each hunting party had returned with little or no success. Those that had traveled east had been gone many days and he feared that tragedy had overtaken them.

Shouts and the barking of the dogs brought him from his musings and he went to investigate the cause of the commotion. The missing hunters had returned at last, ladened with the spoils of the hunt. They told tales of vast herds of animals far to the east toward the ice fields. Tomorrow they would go east in pursuit of this cornucopia of mastodons and mammoths, but tonight, a feast to celebrate the return of good fortune.

The following day they broke camp and headed east and true to their words the herds appeared before them. They stalked the wooly mammoths allowing the dogs to keep them at bay while they plunged their spears deep into these lumbering giants.

As the seasons past the band grew with the plentiful game and the hunter led his people into new territories where the animals had never seen a human being thus falling easy prey to the spears of the hunters.

After many years the hunter, old now and near the end of his life, stood in the pass of a low mountain range and gazed down into a vast basin teeming with wild life. "Yes, this will be a good place to rest," he thought as he signaled his weary band forward. It was a good time to be alive.

Although our hunter had no way of knowing it he led his band into the Old Crow Basin of the northern Yukon. Artifacts found at the site have been dated to 27,000 years ago. The first Canadians had arrived.

*

Some 10,000 years later North America went through a period of warming when the ice sheets began to retreat. The seam where the Cordilleran and Laurentide Sheets came together parted leaving an ice free corridor along the eastern side of the Rockies in present day Alberta through which the descendants of our hunter moved into the interior of North America. Most settled in the more hospitable regions of the southern United States. Here people evolved into complex societies parallel to the rise of European civilizations. But, Canada lay under her blanket of snow and ice for another 10,000 years before her first permanent settlers could share her vast resources. As the weather moderated and the ice sheets began to retreat, Canada's story was about to begin in earnest.

Roughly 12,000 years ago climatic changes saw the warm summer sun melt, not only the precipitation from the previous winter, but also began to work on the accumulated ice and snow from past years. The great glaciers began a slow retreat to the north.

Tonnes of soil, sand and rock, held captive for millennia, were abandoned as the ice lost its grip on them littering the landscape with the features we see today.

In the Maritime Provinces the retreat of the ice brought the return of vegetation in the form of tundra like plants that attracted caribou herds as well as fox, rabbits and myriad other creatures from the New England region and from the east where the continental shelf, now deep within the ocean, was exposed before sea levels rose with the melting ice. Archaeological evidence suggests that circa 10,000 B.C. Palaeo-Indians followed this migration of game and settled the area now known as Nova Scotia, New Brunswick and Prince Edward Island. This group has been identified by the Fluted stone points typical of that era found at several sites including Debert and Cape Blomidon, Nova Scotia; Kingsclear and Quaco Head, New Brunswick and Souris, Prince Edward Island. The major site discovered is at Debert where a number of dwelling places have been unearthed with hearths, which points to a semipermanent settlement. The site is ideally placed to intercept the probable route of migrating caribou from central Nova Scotia, where they summered, to the north in New Brunswick where the wind kept snow cover to a minimum in the winter making food more readily available.

These first human occupants of post glacier Canada lived in simple dome shaped dwellings made with bent poles covered with hides. In winter many layers of skins interspersed with moss and prairie grasses for insulation would have been necessary to keep out the bitter cold of the period. The climate, so close to the retreating ice fields, would have been much more severe than the case today.

Before the seas rose to their present levels it has been speculated that a land bridge existed between the mainland and Prince Edward Island. The depth of the Northumberland Strait supports this hypothesis. The archeological evidence shows that the Palaeo-Indians crossed this land bridge to hunt and settle what became Prince Edward Island.

A strange thing happened shortly after the arrival of these early settlers. Between 8,000 and 3,000 B.C. the evidence of human occupation of the Maritimes disappeared. In Newfoundland and Labrador

**At home in
the Maritimes
c. 8000 B.C.**

occupation is continuous, but the Maritimes seems to have been abandoned. A great debate rages to this day on the reasons. One hypothesis blames the change from open grasslands to forests as the cause. A predominance of pine may have caused large game animals to migrate away from the area and the Palaeo-Indians followed. Another is that the population concentrated along the sea coast to take advantage of the abundance found there. Whatever the explanation there is a mystery for modern historians to solve.

About 3,000 B.C. renewed occupation is in ample evidence. As many as four distinct cultural traits can be established in what has been termed the pre-ceramic era, pre-ceramic indicating the lack of pottery. The Laurentian Tradition is found in northern New Brunswick with significant finds at Dead Man's Pool and Cow Point. This tradition can be linked to similar societies in southern Quebec, northern New York, eastern Ontario and Vermont.

The Maritime Archaic Tradition covered the extreme southern portion of New Brunswick and all of Nova Scotia. These people took their living largely from the sea and evidence has been found embracing land from northern New England to northern Labrador for this group. Unfortunately much of the evidence is now buried beneath the sea.

The third component of the puzzle is the Shield Tradition found primarily at Dead Man's Pool on the Tobique River. Dead Man's Pool was a salmon holding pool where the rich harvest of fish could be easily taken. Another site rich in artifacts of the Shield Tradition is at North Cape, Cape Breton Island. This tradition relates to similar finds in the boreal forests of the Canadian Shield close to Hudson Bay.

The last is another mystery for historians to sort out. It is the Susquehanna Tradition found from Teacher's Cove to Portland Point in New Brunswick.

The mystery is how a culture with roots in the south, especially along the Susquehanna River in Pennsylvania, came to find its way to Atlantic Canada? The Susquehanna people differed from the other Maritime dwellers in that they cremated their dead and buried them in pits with red ochre and goods typical of this tradition.

The first indication of pottery in the Maritimes comes about 750 B.C. Two distinct cultures emerged and correspond to the modern aboriginal peoples that populated the Maritimes at the time of the European exploration. The Micmac were the dominant culture occupying all of Prince Edward Island, northern New Brunswick and most of Nova Scotia. The Malecite settled in the southeastern part of New Brunswick and southwestern Nova Scotia across the Bay of Fundy. Both peoples spoke an Algonkian dialect and could understand each other albeit with difficulty.

This period saw the introduction of clay pots to the area. Previous to that heated rocks were dropped into bark or skin vessels to boil water. The big disadvantage with clay for a nomadic people was their bulk and fragility. Subsequently evidence shows that the old methods continued to be used despite the convenience of clay.

The Micmac were a nomadic people who lived in the interior in fall and winter, moving to the bays and river mouths in spring to take advantage of the fish and sea mammals available there. Migratory birds were also a part of the diet of the early Indian inhabitants.

In late fall when the food supply on the coast became scarce the different bands would disperse into the interior to hunt moose, caribou and smaller game to sustain themselves over the long winter months. The Micmacs also hunted beaver by draining the ponds, thus exposing the lodges making the beaver easy prey to the bow and arrow. If the weather remained good in late winter food would be plentiful but, starvation was always a constant threat if prolonged or deep snow prevailed.

These people were the ancestors of those that greeted the first Europeans to Canada's shores.

*

When the great glacier swept across Newfoundland and Labrador it stripped the land of its top soil, but, unlike the rest of the continent, however, the ice sheet pushed some five hundred kilometres out to sea. As the glaciers began to melt they dropped this rich cache of soil and rock into the ocean. Thus, when the ice sheet withdrew it left a rocky, barren landscape with a thin layer of earth that showed little promise for anything but trees and berries. As if to compensate those that would eventually settle this land the great store of soil dumped into the ocean formed the Grand Banks of Newfoundland, an underwater garden that teems with the fruits of the sea.

As we have seen, when the ice sheets retreated great herds of game animals followed and they in turn were followed by the Archaic Indians who hunted them. As the climate of the Maritimes moderated and gave way to forests the caribou moved on north. About 7000 B.C. the Archaic Indians followed the herds across the mouth of the St. Lawrence River working their way into southern Labrador.

By 5500 B.C. the Indian migrants had settled along the coast and their culture resembled that of the Maritime Archaic Culture of the Maritime Provinces. They lived by hunting and fishing; spreading along the coast as far north as Saglek Bay.

A large concentration of archeological evidence has been found at L'Anse Amour in southern Labrador and at Port au Choix across the Strait of Belle Isle in Newfoundland. The Indians that settled in southern Labrador fished the sea and hunted seals on the spring ice so we can assume that they visited Newfoundland very early in their occupation of the area. The first permanent settlements in Newfoundland occurred about 3000 B.C. Evidence shows a considerable level of sophistication. An elaborate set of bone sewing instruments were found at Port au Choix along with a comb made of caribou antler in the shape of a merganser duck and a beautiful sculpted killer whale carved from igneous rock. They also had developed an ingenious toggled harpoon, which enabled them to hold sea mammals after the initial wound. These early settlers were the ancestors of the Beothuck Indians of Newfoundland and the Naskapi-Montagnais of Labrador.

About 2000 B.C. the lives of the Archaic Indians of Labrador were threatened by the arrival from the north of a completely different race, the Archaic Eskimos.

Stalking caribou in Labrador c. 3000 B.C.

These were descendants of that first group of hunters that crossed the land bridge from Siberia some 30,000 years ago. Over a period covering hundreds of years these Eskimos pushed south and reached Hamilton Inlet before fading into history.

This may have accounted for the decline of the Archaic Indians, however, a further explanation can be found in the infant mortality rate. Half the skeletons found at Port au Choix were of children under two years old. It would be difficult for any culture to survive such dramatic losses for long.

With the disappearance of the Archaic Eskimos another group of the same people, the Dorset Eskimos, arrived occupying Labrador and the west coast of Newfoundland. They arrived on the island about 500 B.C. and mysteriously disappeared from the archeological record about 600 A.D. Along the Labrador coast they survived until 1500 A.D.

Artifacts of the Dorset culture included miniature carvings of the animals that were hunted, amulets and masks. Human figurines were also occasionally made. The discovery of a soapstone carving of a polar bear at Saglet Bay has shown that the bears had a great religious significance to the Dorsets. Their religion is thought to have been animistic in nature believing that all human and animal life are governed by spirits.

The first signs of the Naskapi-Montagnais Indians in Labrador is seen about 600 A.D. Originally they settled along the coast as had their Archaic ancestors. Eventually they migrated to the forbidding interior perhaps due to pressure from the more aggressive Dorset Eskimos. They lived year round in the interior hunting caribou and other game abundant in the area. Artifacts indicate a simple culture as seen by the stone tools uncovered in recent times. They did, however, have a definite flair for intricate decorations of their clothing and footwear.

Four hundred years earlier in 200 A.D. the Beothuck Indians appeared in Newfoundland. They were probably descended from the earlier Archaic Indians as some of their customs were similar such as the use of red ochre in burials. Interestingly enough, unlike their Labradorian cousins, they appeared to have coexisted with the Dorset Eskimos. Evidence indicates that they lived on the coast continuously from 200 to 750 A.D. They lived on the resources of the sea and seashore taking fish, seals and birds for food and shelter. Seal and whale oil supplied both fuel and light. In winter they moved to the interior to hunt caribou, the meat of which they smoked to preserve.

In winter they lived in large communal log houses. These were multi-sided at the base with a cone shaped top arrangement of poles covered with birch bark and moss. In contrast their summer dwellings were flimsy affairs of poles covered with skins or bark. They proved to be skilled with the bow and arrow, the spear and the harpoon.

The Beothuck used birch bark extensively in their day to day lives. Not only did they use it in building shelter but also for canoes and in their art work. Toy birch bark canoes as well as skin moccasins have been discovered in the burial sites of children.

Sometime before the end of the first millennium it was probably a group of Beothuck who saw a strange vessel enter a northern bay. They may have been the first to see the Vikings, that first European contact with Canadian shores.

*

When the Archaic Indians crossed the mouth of the St. Lawrence in pursuit of the great caribou herds many turned southwest along the great river instead of following their cousins into Labrador and Newfoundland. By 4000 B.C. people of the Laurentian Culture occupied southern Quebec, northern New York and Vermont. Important Laurentian sites have been found in the Ottawa Valley particularly on Morrison Island and Allumette Island north of Pembroke, Ontario.

These Laurentian people were displaced by the Shield Archaic Indians, ancestors of the Algonkian tribes, who slowly migrated down from the Keewatin District of the Northwest Territories over hundreds of years. These may have been the first to build birch

bark canoes to help in their quest for food.

As the barren landscape gave way to forests the Woodland Period ushered in the Laurel Culture, which learned the art of pottery making, probably from the people who occupied Southern Ontario. Much of their culture mirrored the experiences of the Indians of Southern Ontario described below.

While the Palaeo-Indians of New England followed the herds of game animals into the Maritimes, Newfoundland and Labrador their cousins living south of the Great Lakes were pushing into Southern Ontario. Bands of hunters stalked caribou across the grass lands that was Ontario in 9000 B.C.

As the ice fields retreated the landscape that greeted these early pioneers was much different than what we see today. In fact it was much different than the pre-glacier scene. When the glacier dragged its debris over the land it filled in the original drainage system. In the Niagara Peninsula the Erigan Channel with its many tributaries was 3.2 kilometres wide with present day Lowbanks, Ontario on its western edge. It ran north past Fonthill, Thorold and St. Catharines to Lake Ontario. When the ice sheet withdrew the glacier lake called Tonawanda dictated that the new drainage system would be further east and the Niagara River was born.

With the ice rapidly melting the flow of water became a force to be reckoned with. The St. Lawrence basin was still plugged with ice and the waters formed large glacier lakes. Lake Iroquois covered a vast area with its northern shoreline the retreating glacier to the north of Toronto and the Niagara Escarpment as its southern shore. The level of Lake Iroquois reached just 35 metres below Queenston Heights before the opening of the St. Lawrence allowed it to recede to the present levels of Lake Ontario. Lake Algonquin covered an area to the north which encompassed Lakes Huron, Michigan and Georgian Bay. Its shore line was approximately 15 kilometres inland from the shores of the lakes today

The Palaeo-Indians bands frequented the shores of the post glacier lakes to intercept the migrating herds of caribou. They lived in small groups roaming the grasslands in search of the animals that fed, clothed and sheltered them.

About 7500 B.C. forests began to take hold across southwestern Ontario giving way to the Archaic Period when the great caribou herds moved north leaving the indigenous people with deer and moose as their primary source of food and shelter. Fishing became important in the survival of the bands and the hunters became skilled at spearing fish, which were then dried to help them through the long harsh winters. As occurred in the east the bands moved inland to hunt during the winter and gathered in larger groups in the spring to fish along the mouths of the rivers.

There was a concentration of settlements around London, Ontario as early as 8000 B.C. No less than forty-three Late Archaic sites have been identified including a significant number around Matthews Woods. Large stemmed stone spear points were found here as well as smaller side notched points. A large bog is one of the features of the Matthews Woods Site.

The Archaic Period ended about 1000 B.C. with the introduction of the Early Woodland Period. Although little changed in the habits of the people, this period saw the introduction of ceramics into Ontario. It is at this time that the bow and arrow was introduced to the area. The beginnings of more social and community identification appeared among the various groups that came together for the spring fishing. This was the forerunner of the later Woodland Period, which saw the rise of the Iroquoian confederacies of which the Iroquois and Huron were the most prominent.

Although there is some evidence of the occupation of the London site in this period, especially around the Matthews Woods site, it appears that the concentration seen in the Archaic Period in that area had diminished. Perhaps the retreat of Lake Algonquin forced the population to move further north and east leaving smaller bands to sustain themselves on the Thames River.

This Early Woodland Period shows evidence of more elaborate burial rituals. Red ochre, used in Labrador and Newfoundland, made its appearance in the burial practices of the Early Woodland Indians. Artifacts found in these burial sites show an increased interest in art as well as evidence of trade. Art made from native copper from the Lake Superior region has been found by archaeologists as well as marine shell pendants and beads from the Atlantic region. Ground

slate figurines indicates a high degree of skill among the ancestors of the Iroquoian group of First Nations.

The Middle Woodland Period began about 400 B.C. and is marked by an increase in the complexity of the social interaction of the various Indian bands and the beginning of the development of distinctive tribal identification. This also marked an increase in the population around the London area once again. Evidence of the continent wide trade system, which was in full flower when the Europeans arrived in the area can be seen in the variety of foreign goods found. Arrowheads made from flint found only in Ohio have turned up along with silver from Northern Ontario and stone tools and panpipes from Illinois.

Toward the end of this period, about 800 C.E., the introduction of corn initiated significant changes in the culture of the people. In this period corn was more of a supplement to the diet rather than a staple item. Hunting and gathering was still the principal means of survival.

The Late Woodland Period, with its explosion of social and political complexity began about the time that the Norsemen of Greenland and Iceland were casting their eyes west across the great unknown sea.

*

In the prairies the great Laurentian Ice Sheet retreated before the relentless pursuit of the sun revealing a vast, flat landscape of grasslands teeming with giant bison and wooly mammoths that fell easy prey to the roving bands of hunters that arrived in southern Alberta and Saskatchewan about 11,500 years ago. The first known site of human habitation in Alberta was found at Vermilion Lakes in present day Banff National Park. These hunters camped on the slope of Mount Edith about 8500 B.C. and left a wealth of archeological evidence for us to ponder. Bones of bison and a now extinct species of big horn sheep were scattered about the camp along with stone tools called bifaces, which were sharpened on both sides and likely used for butchering. The shelters built by these early explorers were made of poles covered with skins much as did the Palaeo-Indians of the east.

About this time the great Pleistocene mammals, mastodons, wooly mammoths and myriad other species, vanished from the land. Scientists still debate the cause of their demise. It is doubtful that the small bands of Palaeo-Indians could have hunted them to extinction, so the mystery continues.

Unlike eastern Canada the southern parts of Alberta and Saskatchewan did not move from grassland to boreal forests. The hunter/gatherers did not evolve into an agricultural society as did those in Ontario. They roamed the plains constantly moving as they followed the great herds of giant bison, which provided their food, shelter and clothing.

How did these early inhabitants manage to hunt these great beasts on foot and with just their spears to kill their prey? An archeological dig at the Fletcher site in Alberta gives us a look at one method. While digging a water hole for cattle a large quantity of bones were uncovered along with spear points at what was once a spring fed slough. The marshy ground made for slow going for the great bison and the hunters would surround the small herd as they drank. The hunters moved in and killed as many as they could before they were able to escape to firmer ground where their speed made hunting difficult.

After the kill the women would butcher the animals where they fell leaving many spear points in the water and mud to be discovered 10,000 years later by an enterprising Alberta rancher and amateur archaeologist. Another method was the buffalo jump. The seemingly endless plains are dotted here and there with bluffs that were utilized by the hunters in their struggle for survival. One such bluff in Alberta is known as Head-Smashed-In Buffalo Jump.

The medicine men and women, dressed in buffalo skins and feather headdresses, call on the Great Spirit to bless the hunt. An Iniskim (a small buffalo shaped stone) is tossed in the air and caught in a hide blanket to mimic the hunt. If it works the buffalo will fall to their deaths. The fate of 200 hunters and their families depend on the magic.

For three days the "buffalo runners" have stalked the herd in the treeless Porcupine hills some ten kilometres from the jump. Skilled in working the herd they carefully try to maneuver the great beasts toward the waiting hunters.

A runner, a wolf skin draped over his head and body, spots a calf straying in the direction of the jump. He quickly mimics the wolf and harasses the calf forcing the adults to come to its rescue and edging ever closer to the hunters waiting to begin the stampede. The runners had checked the drive lanes three days earlier to be sure that all was ready.

The drive lanes were piles of stones used to mark the route to the jump. Over 100 hunters were responsible for keeping the stampeding herd within those lanes.

The runner harassing the calf allowed a smile as he heard the bleating of another calf further along calling for its mother. Another runner more skilled than he has disguised himself as a calf and now the entire herd was moving toward him. Soon now the moment of true would come. Would the great beasts stay in the lanes? Would they suddenly change direction and trample the hunters under foot? So many things could go wrong. He knew that this was a precise operation. The buffalo had to hit a 100 metre stretch of the bluff if the hunt was to be successful.

The herd begins to move. The time for stealth is passed. The runners begin to wave their disguises and yell. The pace picks up. As the herd enters the drive lanes more hunters appear waving hide blankets and screaming at the top of their lungs. The lead bull tries to turn, but a flash of a blanket swings him back. The medicine men chant. The hunters scream. The herd pounds on.

Now the physical shape of the bison are against them as they begin the downhill run to the jump. Their short back legs can't handle the massive front weight. Only the dozen or so buffalo at the front of the herd can see where they are going. Suddenly the lead bull realizes the danger and attempts to stop. The momentum of those behind pushes him over the edge and the entire herd follows dropping fifteen metres to the waiting hunters below. The slaughter begins.

The exhausted runner and his companions rush to the scene watching for any strays that may have escaped. None must be allowed to survive because they will tell the other buffalo of the trap and future herds will avoid it.

Another successful hunt ensured the survival of the band. The buffalo were butchered with nothing going to waste. The hide was cut away quickly to promote cooling thus preventing spoilage. The bulk of the meat was dried and made into pemmican, a mixture of animal fat, meat and berries that were stored in hide containers for the winter months.

Head-Smashed-In was one of several jumps scattered across the prairies. They are a tribute to the ingenuity of the early hunters of the plains. About 2000 B.C. Head-Smashed-In was mysteriously abandoned as a jump for about a thousand years. Could it be that a buffalo escaped and the word got out to the other herds?

**Head-
Smashed-In
buffalo jump
c. 2500 B.C.**

About 1000 B.C. a new people appeared on the scene. They have been identified by the style of projectile points discovered at Pelican Lake in southern Saskatchewan. They represent a renaissance on the plains with their broadened contact with other hunting groups. Tools from Montana and Wyoming as well as their use of the tipi mark them from the hunters that came before them.

At the beginning of the first century C.E. another group, the Besant culture, inhabited the plains from Manitoba to the rockies. They were excellent bison hunters and used the old jumps extensively. They often used spear tips made from Knife River flint found only in the Dakotas. About the time that the Vikings were sailing west another group called the Avonlea culture introduced the bow and arrow to the plains. With the comings and goings of each aboriginal civilization the people remained the hunters and gatherers of the plains.

*

The first humans to traverse British Columbia probably were the direct descendants of those hunters that crossed the land bridge from Siberia 31,000 years ago. The ice free corridor that eventually allowed people to move south into the United States cut the northeast corner of the province east of the Rockies.

As the Cordilleran Ice Sheet withdrew into the mountains it left behind cold rivers that were often dammed by ice. This resulted in flooded valleys and large glacier lakes. One of the largest was Peace Lake east of the Rockies. Lakes Okanagan, Nichols and Shuswap are remnants of these glacier lakes today.

The oldest site yet discovered is in the Peace River district of northeastern British Columbia where the Charlie Lake Cave site goes back 10,500 years. The hunter/gatherers that occupied the area hunted many of the same animals as their prairie cousins, but using a different method. Instead of open grasslands, rocky draws and mountain streams greeted the stalkers of big game.

The hunters crouch along the sandstone slope as the herd of bison approaches the far side of the narrows of Peace Lake. The lead bull pauses at the water's edge testing the air for any sign of danger. The hunters hold their breath. The least bit of noise will send the herd stampeding in the opposite direction. The Bull, satisfied, plunges into the lake and lunges up the gravel beach beneath the waiting spears. Other bulls appear followed by the cows and then the young and old. They stand dripping and steaming on the shore for a brief moment before following the bull inland.

The ambush spot has been chosen well. The bison must pass between two sheer rock outcrops and it is here that the hunters strike. With a shout they leap up from their hiding places above the herd spears poised for the kill. The waving and yelling stampedes the herd, but some bison begin milling around in confusion, trapped between the rock faces. Spears bite deep into the shaggy hides of the bison and when the dust settles six bison carcasses lay crumbled in the rocky draw. The men immediately begin the task of butchering and soon the women will join the group to pack and preserve their lifeline to survival.

On the west side of the Rockies the retreating glaciers left the coast open for human habitation. The great weight of the ice had crushed the land mass leaving the shoreline much different than it is today. As the continent rebounded the shoreline was pushed west. The heavily glaciated Fraser Valley, for example, was still depressed enough 12,000 years ago to allow an arm of the sea over 150 metres deep to penetrate far inland. A small barbed antler harpoon head was found at Glenrose now 20 kilometres from the sea. Glenrose was at the mouth of the river at the time of the earliest occupation.

Nine thousand years ago the sea had dropped ten metres rising again about 5,000 years ago. In contrast, the Queen Charlotte Islands experienced sea levels 30 metres below present levels allowing these now isolated islands to be colonized by the ancient ancestors of those that live there today. The sea rose to heights ten to fifteen metres above present levels before falling back about 5,000 years ago.

Archeological evidence places human occupation of the coastal areas for at least 10,000 years. Large quantities of pebble tools have been discovered in the Fraser Valley. These tools were made from rounded,

fist sized pebbles found on the beaches and river bottoms. The one side had flakes knocked off to form a strong cutting edge while the other side was left smooth to fit the hand. These ancient tools were used for heavy cropping as well as cutting and scrapping wood, fibre and meat.

The early seagoing culture of the Queen Charlottes used skin or bark canoes. The hunters used stone micro blades as points to hunt sea lions and seals. In contrast the Fraser Valley inhabitants used a different tool kit consisting of leaf shaped spearheads and knives. Evidence shows that salmon was important in the diet of the coastal Indians. Netted salmon were dried in the warm canyon winds that blow down the Fraser Valley.

Traces of the Old Cordilleran Culture can be found around the Strait of Georgia as far as the northern end of Vancouver Island and up the Fraser River as far as the canyon. Evidence showed that these people engaged in long distance trading. Obsidian, a volcanic glass, desired because of the sharp cutting edge it yielded, has been traced to the Oregon coast some 700 kilometres to the south.

In what is called the middle developmental period the use of the great cedar trees of the coast comes into evidence. The master builder would carefully select his tree and after cutting it down would begin the process of splitting and carving. Wooden and antler wedges were driven with stone hammers to split the pliable red cedar. Cedar was used to build houses as well as the great seagoing canoes that greeted the first Europeans to visit the area. The advent of the large canoes greatly expanded the ability of the people to trade over vast distances.

The people of the coast began consuming large amounts of shell fish about 5,000 years ago. Deep shell middens have been found at Glenrose near Vancouver and Namu. Thick accumulations of mussel and clam shells mixed with the floor sweepings of ancient dwellings tell an intriguing tale of prehistory on the shores of British Columbia.

*

Although the first humans to come to Canada crossed Beringia into Alaska and the Yukon some 30,000 years ago the high Arctic east of the Yukon remained the dominion of the polar bears and seals for

Hunting the Great White Bear c. 1000 B.C.

some 25,000 years. Indian hunters from the south may have followed the migrating caribou herds north of the tree line in summer but would have retreated to the south at the onset of the long arctic night.

Circa 3000 B.C.. the Palaeo-Eskimos began to migrate east into the barren peninsulas and desolate islands that was the high Arctic. Whether driven there by more aggressive peoples or simply by the call of the unknown will never be determined, but this strong and gentle race of nomads lived the year round on the Arctic coast and tundra.

The Palaeo-Eskimos lived in tents comprised of light poles covered with skins. the poles were cut from drift wood or brought up from the forests of the south. In winter the sides of the tents would have been banked with snow to insulate the dwelling against the cold winds. The floor plan of the interior resembles that of the Eurasian pattern. A central box hearth formed part of a central corridor down the middle of the tent. On either side of this corridor was the sleeping and working areas. The Eurasian models used logs to form the corridor while the early Eskimos used slabs of rock for the same purpose.

The archeological evidence of these dwellings is remarkably in tact. The fact that the population was so small and scattered combined with the location of the tents on the Arctic beaches has left the remains undisturbed for 4,000 years. The Arctic islands, crushed for millennia under the weight of the great glaciers, were slowly rising up, thus the beaches were constantly being renewed. Rarely was the same site used twice and even if another group happened on the same place some years later the old location was no longer on the beach. Subsequently archaeologists can view the floor plan as if it were constructed yesterday.

These Palaeo-Eskimos lived by hunting sea mammals with harpoons attached to retrieving lines.

Barbed bone spears first developed by Siberian fishermen were used in fishing and hunting birds. They also brought the bow and arrow with them from their ancestors in northern Asia. Life was hard and precarious for these nomadic people who usually traveled in small groups or single families. Starvation was constantly at their door as well as the ever present danger that comes with sharing the landscape with the mighty polar bear. In the winter months families were always on the move in search of game or seals to ensure survival for another day. Everything from food and shelter to fuel came from the animals they hunted.

The family settled down in their new location as the wind whipped around the snow banked tent. There was an air of resignation permeating the interior. They had killed a great white bear the day before, but, they had been driven off by the arrival of another bear with her half grown cubs. Food was at a critical low and fuel to feed the hearth would soon run out.

Despite this the young hunter was well satisfied with his efforts. He had made a tunnel of snow blocks at the entrance to the tent, which kept out the draft. A chance meeting with another family that summer had made him aware of the technique.

Suddenly the dogs began to bark outside and the entire family became alert. The fear was almost visible as the hunters reached for their bows and spears. Was it the mate of the great white bear they had killed the previous day come for revenge? They had stumbled upon the bear quite by accident and it had attacked. It had been a close thing. Two dogs were killed before the bear went down. But for the intrusion by the female bear there would now be plenty of food and fuel.

Scrambling out of the tent the hunters mood swung from one of apprehension to one of joy. A herd of musk oxen had wandered too close to the camp and the dogs now had them in their defensive circle. Fortune smiled on them this night.

The hunters went to work with bows and spears and before the herd finally stampeded away several animals lay still in the blood covered snow. The women and children rushed out to help with the butchering. Food for several weeks and great robes to ward off the Arctic cold would sustain the band through most of the winter. For the first time in days the sound of laughter drifted from the tent as the children played and the hearth fire flamed anew.

The Palaeo-Eskimos continued to migrate east and eventually reached the Labrador coast. Between 950 C.E. and the coming of the Europeans the Palaeo-Eskimos disappeared from the landscape. Speculation is that the more aggressive ancestors of the Inuit that now occupy the north invaded the high Arctic from Alaska and drove them to extinction.

Though they are extinct the Palaeo-Eskimos left their mark on Canada and indeed the rest of North America. They introduced the bow and arrow to the continent as well as showing the Inuit that followed them that it was possible to live and to thrive in an almost impossible climate.

The Palaeo-Eskimo's life was not all drudgery. Among the hearth stones and fragments of bones scattered about their camps pieces of art have been found. The artisan selected brightly coloured stones and chipped them with a skill that is hard to match in the ancient world. Miniature tools were jewel like in their composition. Bone and ivory carvings are also uncovered from time to time in the endless search for the ancient people of the north.

VINLAND THE GOOD

" It is called Vinland because vines spring up wild there, bearing excellent grapes. Beyond that island there is no habitable land to be found in the ocean, everything beyond it is full of impenetrable ice and utter darkness." Norse Sagas

Before we meet the first Europeans to visit Canada it is important to know something of who they were. The Vikings of Denmark, Norway and Sweden were the scourge of Europe for almost 300 years beginning in about 790 C.E.. until 1050. Viking warriors raided and pillaged over vast expanses of ocean, wherever their long ships would carry them. Their warships, called drekars (dragons) swept out of the morning mist along some peaceful coast to decimate yet another sleepy village.   Who could forget the tales of King Æthelred the Unready of England who paid the Norsemen the Danegeld to make peace in 994 A.D.

However, The Vikings were more than raiders. They were explorers constantly in search of new lands to settle in peace and freedom. Unlike the drekars their trading vessels, called knorrs, were broad of beam for maximum cargo capacity. The knorr was basically an open boat in which animals, cargo and possessions were tied down amidships to maintain the trim. The bulwarks were high to keep out the water in all but the heaviest seas. In 825 A.D. they colonized the Faroes Islands to the north of Scotland. In 870 a vast empty island to the west was sighted by two different Viking ships one commanded by Gardar of Sweden and the other by Naddod of Faroe. Some 20 years later the first brave settlers from Norway sailed to build a new life on the wind swept shores of Iceland.

The burly Norseman at the steering oar watched the gathering clouds, making a mental note to get the covers over the livestock and casks. He would wait as long as possible to give the oxen as much daylight as he could for once it began to blow in earnest it might be days before they could remove the protective cover. He glanced down the length of his ship as his family began preparations for the coming storm.   Despite the rough seas the knorr was handling well and would get them through.

A gust of wind was his signal and a wave of his hand sent everyone, men, women and children, to the task of battening down the ship. The cattle and horses stomped about nervously as the knorr met the heavy seas. Rain began to fall and soon became a wind driven deluge. For three days the bailing buckets were in constant use as the waves broke over the high bulwarks of this sturdy Viking

vessel.

On the third day the wind slackened and by midday the covers came off and the weary family took their first rest. Soon their new home came into view and all praised Aegir, god of the sea, for their safe arrival.

By 930 A.D. over 20,000 people inhabited Iceland, which had its own parliament called the Althing. It was from here that the Viking sailors explored "west over seas" as the Norse sagas called it.

In 900 A.D. Gunnbjorn Ulfsson's ship was driven past Iceland in a gale and he sighted the barren coast of Greenland. He retraced his steps back to Iceland, but the sighting he made became part of the Norse oral history and led to the next step in the discovery of Canada.

Some eighty years later Thorvald Asvaldson and his son Erik the Red were exiled from Iceland for constantly feuding with their neighbours. They decided to explore the land that Gunnbjorn had sighted. Landing at a place they called Erik's Island. They wintered there spending the next three years exploring this vast coastline. To help persuade as many Icelanders as possible to emigrate to this new colony he named it Greenland. In 986 he set sail with 25 ships. It was a rough passage and only 14 ships arrived. Some turned back to Iceland and some were lost at sea.

Despite the harsh conditions the Greenland colony flourished. Game was plentiful and the fjords were teeming with fish. Regular vessels from Iceland brought them corn, wood and iron for which they traded polar bear pelts, ivory from walrus tusks and rope woven from walrus skin.

One of the leaders who followed Erik to Greenland was Herjolf Bardarson. His son Bjarni Herjolfsson was away when his father sailed for Greenland and on his return to Iceland decided to follow his father west. Three days out he ran into fog and strong northerly winds driving him beyond his destination. Several

The Vikings
Cross the
Northern Sea
c. 900 C.E.

days passed before the sun reappeared and he was able to take bearings. The following day he sighted land. It was low lying, with wooded hills.. Bjarni was sure this could not be Greenland. He put out to sea again landing at his father's farm in Greenland some seven days later. Although he did not realize it Bjarni was the first European to see the shores of Canada.

Bjarni settled down in Greenland to farm, but, Leif, son of Erik the Red, was determined to follow up on the sighting of this new land. He visited Bjarni and after some discussion bought his ship, raised a crew of 35 men, and sailed west on a great adventure.

The first sight of land was a bleak slab of rock capped by a great glacier. It is hard to determine the location, but by the description in the Norse sagas it was likely the southern tip of Baffin Island. Leif landed there and named it Helluland or "Slab-Land" after its huge slabs of bare rock. They returned to their ship and headed south.

They sighted land again and knew that this was the land that Bjarni had sighted, low lying and wooded. White sandy beaches greeted the Vikings when they landed. By its description this was probably the coast of Labrador. The well forested interior would provide Greenland with much needed timber and Leif named it Markland or "Forest-Land" because of its vast wood resources.

After a brief landing at Markland Leif continued south landing again somewhere between the Gulf of St. Lawrence and the New Jersey coast. We know from the Norse sagas that there was salmon in the river where they wintered and salmon is not usually found south of the Hudson River in New York State. One of Leif's men discovered vines bearing wild grapes thus Leif named this place Vinland or "Wine-Land". During the return voyage to Greenland Leif earned the

15

nickname Leif the Lucky when he rescued 15 shipwrecked sailors in the spring of 988.

Like Bjarni, Leif the Lucky chose not to return to Vinland, but as the stories were told in the long winter nights in a Greenland fjord the yearning for adventure stirred in the heart of Leif's brother Thorvald who looked west with its promise of new lands and new sagas.

*

As the stories of Vinland the Good were woven into the tapestry of Norse legend Thorvald Eriksson was determined to follow his brother leif's example and sail west in search of adventure. Leif enthusiastically endorsed his plan and gave him the same ship that he and Bjarni had used. Rounding up a crew of 30 Thorvald sailed for Vinland in 989 A.D.

With the directions given him by his brother, Thorvald made his landfall and found the huts that Leif had built. These were appropriately named "Leif's Houses" and Thorvald used them as a base camp for two summers of exploration along the Vinland coast. In the second summer a fateful encounter occurred between the Vikings and the local aboriginal people.

The knorr entered the peaceful bay on yet another day of new discoveries in this wondrous land. As they rounded the point the lookout called Thorvald's attention to the small fleet of skin boats pulling out from the shore. Thorvald took note of the bows and clubs carried by the warriors and without a word being spoken each of his men moved closer to their own weapons. They had encountered many of the native peoples of Vinland and their reception ranged from polite to cool, but no open conflicts had occurred to date. When the boats split up to come at the knorr from both sides the Vikings picked up their axes and swords and prepared for battle. An arrow thumped into the gunwale and with a shout the natives moved to the attack. Fighting was vicious and Thorvald was everywhere rallying his men. He rushed from one crisis point to another as the boarders were repelled only to make gains elsewhere.

Finally the natives had enough and broke off their attack paddling frantically for shore. Many bodies floated face down in the sea as a testament to the valor of the Viking warriors. The Vikings cheered and shouted barbs at their retreating enemy.

The cheers and back slapping came to a sudden halt as they turned to congratulate their leader. Thorvald sat with his back against the mast, an arrow stuck deep in his chest.

They rushed forward, but Thorvald raised his hand and shook his head. All knew that the wound was a fatal one.

Thorvald Eriksson, brother of Leif the Lucky, was the first European to be buried beneath the soil of this new land. His men named those that had attacked them Skraelings or "savage wretches" because of the sad loss of their leader.

Thorvald's crew spent the winter in Vinland and then sailed for Greenland with a cargo of grapes and vines. On arrival they were greeted by the news of the death of Erik the Red. The saga of Vinland was added to around the fires of the Greenland colony.

Thorstein Eriksson, the third son of Erik, was determined to sail to Vinland and bring his brother's body home. He sailed from Greenland with his wife Gudrid and a crew of 25, but never reached Vinland. The voyage was plagued by contrary winds and gales that drove them back to Greenland. Shortly thereafter Thorstein and many of his crew died of a mysterious illness.

Despite the misfortune that befell these voyages, talk of Vinland the Good persisted. Plans were put into place to establish a permanent settlement in the land of grapes and vast forests. The leader of this new enterprise was Thorfinn Karlsefni, a wealthy Norwegian, who arrived in Greenland the summer after the death of Thorstein Eriksson. Thorfinn married Thorstein's widow Gudrid and lived for a time with Leif the Lucky at his farm at Brattahid.

Some time between 998 and 1000 A.D. Thorfinn set sail with 60 men and five women, and a wide variety of farm animals, one of which was a bull for breeding. This voyage was successful and they landed at Erik's Houses to set up their homes. The animals were turned out to pasture and they made preparations to pass their first winter in Canada. Thorfinn was first and foremost a shrewd business man and he ordered timber to by cut and dried for sale in wood starved Greenland. He saw a great opportunity for regular trade with their kin across the sea.

After spending a peaceful winter the spring brought a new menace to the fledgling colony. The Skraelings made an appearance as the balmy days of summer approached. At first there was hope of peace between

Landing on
the
Newfoundland
coast
c. 1000 C.E.

he colonists and the Skraelings. The natives were anxious to trade furs for milk from the Viking's cattle.

Thorfinn distrusted the Skraelings from his first meeting with them. He especially frowned on their interest in steel weapons. He gave strict orders that no weapons were to be traded. It was not long before a skraeling was killed attempting to steal weapons from the colony. Thorfinn knew that an armed attack was soon to come and the Viking warriors prepared to defend their homes.

When the fight came the natives unleashed a secret weapon that the Vikings had never seen. A heavy stone was catapulted from the end of a pole causing havoc among the defenders. The battle raged and two Vikings were killed by Skraeling arrows and clubs, but four Skraelings fell before the swords and battle axes of the Norsemen. The Skraelings had the advantage of numbers, but it was a battle between the Stone Age and the Iron Age and in the end the natives retreated.

One of the fleeing warriors picked up the axe of one of the slain Vikings and stopped to chop at a tree with it. Each member of the war party took a turn and they were much impressed by it sharpness. One tried it out on a rock and the blade broke. He discarded the axe. What good was a tool if it could not withstand stone?

The colony was left in peace that winter, but in the spring Thorfinn gathered his people and announced that there was no hope of founding a permanent settlement. The colonists were too few in number and the Skraelings would never leave them in peace. Packing a wide variety of produce including vines, grapes and furs, they set sail for Greenland and faded into Norse legend.

In 1121 the Bishop of Greenland, Erik Gnupsson, sailed for Vinland to convert the Skraelings of Norse legend to Christianity. The last of the Viking voyagers, he was never seen again.

THE VOYAGES OF JOHN CABOT

"to seek out, discover and find whatsoever islands,continents, regions and provinces of the heathens and infidels in whatever part of the world they be, which before this time have been unknown to all Christians." Letters Patent of John "Caboote"

After the return of Thorfinn Karlsefni to Greenland circa 1003 A.D. Vinland faded into the netherworld of Norse legend. In 1121 the Bishop of Greenland, Erik Gnupsson, sailed for Vinland to convert the Skraelings of Norse legend to Christianity. The last of the Viking voyagers, he was never seen again.

North America lay in obscurity for 489 years. It was to take a pair of Genoese navigators to rekindle the European interest in the legend of Vinland.

Christopher Columbus and Giovanni Caboto were each born in Genoa circa 1450. Little is known of their early lives, however, it is possible that they knew each other in their youth. When Giovanni was ten years old his father, a wealthy merchant named Guilo Caboto, moved his family to Venice. Giovanni was granted citizenship in the city in 1476 and he married a Venetian woman by the name of Mattea. By 1484 he and Mattea had three sons Lewis, Sebastian and Sanctius.

Caboto earned his living as a real estate agent and merchant. Beginning in 1484 he made several trips to the middle east as a merchant's agent where he earned a reputation as a great navigator and a skilled geographer. He spent the years 1485 to 1490 making runs from Venice to Mecca. During these travels he became convinced that the world was round and the shortest way to the Indies was by sailing west across the great sea.

Sometime after 1490 Giovanni Caboto moved his family to England where he settled in Bristol, the great port that was at the height of its prosperity. The Bristol merchants were among the most aggressive traders in Britain and were in the process of outfitting ships to explore the western ocean. From Bristol English woollen goods were shipped to the known world. It was here that Giovanni Caboto settled to raise his family and expound his view that the way to the riches of Cathay lay to the west across the Atlantic. Sometime in this period, whether by his own design or by the usage of his English neighbours, Giovanni Caboto became known as John Cabot.

The voyage of Christopher Columbus in 1492 gained a new credence for the views of Cabot among the merchants of Bristol. They were not adverse to risk, for they had ventured into the unknown and established trade links with Iceland in 1490. The idea of a western route to Asia was very intriguing indeed. Had not this Christopher Columbus found the midriff of Asia?

King Henry VII, first of the Tudor kings, was anxious to share in the treasures of the east. Letters patent were issued to John "Caboote" and his three sons to set sail with five ships, paid for by their own money, and **"to seek out, discover and find whatsoever islands, continents, regions and provinces of the heathens and infidels in whatever part of the world they be, which before this time have been unknown to all Christians."** They were to raise the flag of England over any new lands they found and to acquire **"dominion, title and jurisdiction over these towns, castles, islands and mainlands so discovered."** The only restrictions given were that they were to stay clear of the southern seas, which the Spanish had already claimed. Henry was not anxious to antaganize his old enemy after the Hundred Years War, which had just ended.

Of course good King Henry covered his bets, so to speak. Although he could suffer no losses due to the venture, the royal treasury was to receive 1/5th of all profits realized by the voyage. In return the Cabots were to receive a monopoly on the trade and Bristol was to be the only port of entry for any ships engaged in the Asian trade. Needless to say all financial risks lay with the merchants of Bristol and John Cabot.

Cabot was only able to muster one ship, but he set sail in 1496 for the Vinland of Norse legend. Troubles plagued the venture from the offset. The Bristol sailors, used to the northern Icelandic route, balked at sailing due west. Food was poor and in short supply and the weather added to the misery of voyage. Little is known of this ill fated attempt to reach the new world, but, whether the crew refused to continue or a combination of crew, food and weather, Cabot was

The Matthew battles the Atlantic

forced to return to Bristol.

Perhaps a brief explanation of the sailors lot in the late 15th century might be useful. The ship that Cabot acquired for his voyage of exploration was a Caravel called the *Matthew*. It would have been about 100 feet long and rigged with three masts. The main and fore masts were square rigged while the mizzen mast (rear) carried a lateen sail (a triangular sail). The crew slept and ate in cramped quarters below decks. A perpetual dampness permeated everything. The sides of the ship would sweat continually, especially in bad weather. The rations were salt pork or beef packed in casks whose quality was never known until the ship was far out to sea. Often the meat was unfit for human consumption. Ships biscuits were brought aboard in great sacks and were soon as hard as rocks and full of weevils. Sailors learned early to tap their biscuits on their mess table before eating. This normally drove the weevils out. Water was another problem. Casks of water soon became rancid and when the bottom of a cask was reached often more maggots than water came up with the ladle.

In stormy weather no one got any rest. An hour might not go by without the call of, "All hands! All hands on deck!" The bare foot sailors would scramble into the tops to shorten sail or take in a reef, fisting the hardened canvas until their fingers bled. Those on deck hauled on ropes as the ship changed tack in all kinds of weather. When they did rest it was swinging in hammocks jammed together between decks. Added to all this was the absolute reliance on the navigator to get them safely through. We can only imagine how the sailors of Bristol felt about following this new comer with the strange accent into the unknown.

Despite this set back Cabot and his backers were determined to succeed and in early May of 1497 John Cabot set sail on the voyage that was to change forever the future of Canada.

**Fishing the
Grand Banks
c. 1500 C.E.**

*

John Cabot stood on the quarterdeck of the "Matthew" as they prepared to get underway. Some of the merchants of Bristol, backers of the voyage, stood on the jetty to watch the vessel make sail as if their presents might be a charm for the success of this voyage to find the fabled riches of the east. Find the route to the east by sailing west Cabot had told them and he planned to do just that.

Cabot listened to the clack, clack of the capstan as the crew put their backs into freeing the anchor from the harbour mud. The cry from the bow, "Up and down," brought everyone to the ready. Cabot checked the pendants. The wind had backed a bit, but not enough to bother the "Matthew" which tugged at her cable as if eager to rid herself of the smell of the land. Men stood at the braces ready to haul when the order came.

"Anchors away!" The ship, free at last, swung wildly in the stiff breeze and for a moment seemed out of control. The crew hauled madly on the braces and, after what seemed like an eternity, she settled in for her run down the Avon to the Bristol Channel and on to the open Atlantic where the great unknown waited.

Cabot sailed with a crew of eighteen, which included two Bristol merchants, fourteen Bristol sailors and two of Cabot's personal friends, a Genoese and a Bergundian who was a barber by trade. The barber was probably brought along to act as surgeon, a role often filled by barbers when doctors were scarce. The two merchants were thought to have been Michael Thorne and Hugh Eliot, two investors in the project, who were along to insure that the Bristol sailors obeyed Cabot's orders avoiding a repeat of the 1496 voyage.

The weather in the Atlantic was fair, but, Cabot ran into contrary winds that slowed his progress. After three weeks at sea they ran into floating ice pans and thick fog that held them back even more. Cabot noted in his log that his compass was reading two "rhumbs" off north. A rhumb was about 11 degrees on a modern compass. He corrected his course and on June 27, 1497 at 5 A.M. the cry of "Land-ho!" rang out from the masthead.

The gloom of four weeks at sea vanished in an

20

instant. Sailors clamoured to the rail to get a glimpse of the fabled orient. Cabot leveled his telescope and surveyed the headland. He named it "Prima Tierra Vista" or Land First Sighted. The exact location of this landfall is not known but it probably was somewhere on the north coast of Newfoundland, probably Cape Bauld.

Cabot realized that the place sighted was too rough for a landing so he turned south and within hours discovered a sheltered harbour surrounded by high hills. Thick forests of evergreens covered the terrain that greeted them.

The "Matthew" dropped anchor and Cabot, with a small party, rowed ashore and, with as much pomp and circumstance as could be mustered in this strange wilderness, planted a cross, the banners of Henry VII of England, the Pope and St. Mark, the patron saint of Venice. He formally took possession of the "New Isle" in the name of King Henry.

The first thing that Cabot noticed was that the sight had recently been occupied by humans. Droppings indicated domesticated animals. They also found a stick a half yard long with holds at both ends and painted with brasil. Because he had so few men with him he did not advance inland for fear of a confrontation. After filling the ship's casks with fresh water he returned to the ship. The report of farm animals may have been Cabot's way of putting the best light on his discovery. Domesticated animals indicated the poor peasant population of Cathay with the treasures yet to be uncovered.

Cabot coasted south and charted as much of the coastline as possible. He covered 950 nautical miles going as far south as Placentia Bay. On entering Placentia Bay he saw only the vast expanse of the Atlantic to the south and west. Had he continued west he would have sighted the the Burin Peninsula, but he turned at that point and, retracing his route, sailed for England.

On his return Cabot was hailed as a hero, he immediately rode to London for an audience with the king who rewarded him with 10 pounds sterling for discovering his "new-founde-lande" as Henry termed

it. Cabot returned to Bristol and basked in the glow of fame. He was the "Grand Admiral" dispensing largesse at a whim. An island to this one and some land to that all in Cathay, the fabled orient.

Plans for a second expedition were immediately set in place. This time five ships were commissioned and in May of 1498 Cabot sailed with 300 men to find the rich cities of Asia. With holds crammed with English woolens, hats and other goods they sailed from Bristol with dreams of wealth and prosperity. In reality the voyage was a failure and is shrouded in mystery to this day.

The expedition's failure lays at the feet of a faulty premise of Cabot's. He was determined to turn north on making his landfall to reach the wealthy cities of the east. On reaching Newfoundland he turned north in search of the Northwest Passage, beginning a quest that lasted for over 400 years. Soon they found themselves sailing amid a sea of icebergs. The weather turned cold, but Cabot pushed on convinced that he was on the right track.

The weather became so cold that the attempt had to be abandoned and Cabot reluctantly turned south again. He was determined not to return to England empty handed and he sailed along the coast in search of some sort of wealth. He got as far south as Cape Breton and Nova Scotia, but the only wealth that filled the holds of his ships was cod from the teeming waters of the Grand Banks.

With his return to Bristol England seemed to lose interest in this "New-Founde-Lande" and no Bristol sailors returned seeking the silks and spices of China. Instead the fishermen of Portugal and Spain came to the Grand Banks to reap the harvest of fish that abounded there, but, aside from seeking shelter in stormy weather no one came to settle the land.

Little is known of John Cabot after that fateful second voyage. Some speculate that he did not return to England at all, but was lost at sea. In any case his pension of 20 pounds was paid in 1498 and 1499, but then it stopped. Did he die in 1499? Did King Henry withdraw the pension? John Cabot rediscovered a continent, but it was to be 36 years before the next serious attempt was made to explore this great land.

THE ABORIGINAL CULTURAL MOSAIC

At the dawn of the European exploration of the North American Continent a diverse cultural mosaic that in many ways was as complex and in some cases more sophisticated than the European models of the day awaited them. Although the aboriginal people did not own the land in the European sense, each tribe did control territory that they considered their hunting grounds and wars were fought to maintain that control or to displace enemies.

In the Maritime provinces and Gaspé on the south shore of the St. Lawrence the Micmac held sway. The Micmac civilization had its own distinct government, education and economic systems. The territory was divided into seven districts consisting of:

Wunama'kik, now Cape Breton Island;

Piwkyuk (where gaseous explosions erupt), representing the area around Pictou, Nova Scotia and all of Prince Edward Island;

Eskikewa'kik (skin dressers' territory), stretching from Guysborough to Halifax Counties, Nova Scotia;

Sipekne'katik (ground nut place), extending over the counties of Halifax, Lunenburg, Kings, Hants and Colchester;

Kespukwitk, including Queens, Shelburne, Yarmouth, Digby and Annapolis Counties;

Siknikt, covering Cumberland County, Nova Scotia and the New Brunswick counties of Westmoreland, Albert, Kent, St. John, Kings and Queens; and

Kespek (the last land), consisting of the territory north of the Richibucto River and those parts of Gaspe not occupied by the Iroquois.

There were three levels of government in the Micmac Nation, the local chief looked after the affairs of the summer village presiding over a council of elders that governed the village. The local chief was responsible for providing dogs for the chase, canoes and emergency food supplies in time of need.

Each district had a chief who was usually the eldest son of the most powerful family. His power came from the size of his family so the chief had several wives. The honour of being the wife of the chief

seems to have kept the incidence of jealousy to a minimum. The district chief headed a council of all the local chiefs who helped him rule his district. The council met twice a year, in the fall and spring resolving issues such as peace and war.

To deal with issues affecting the entire nation, a grand council consisting of all the district chiefs and their families was called. The grand chief presided. He was one of the district chiefs chosen by the grand council to be the nation's spokesman. Peace treaties were ratified and hunting and fishing grounds assigned by this council.

Unlike European monarchs the chiefs among the Micmac humbled themselves both in dress and lifestyle as a sign that the well-being of his people came before his own. He shared his food with the poor, even those from other villages. Whenever he traveled from one village to another he took along gifts of meat and fruit to distribute.

Conservation was an important part of the Micmac government. Moose, the main source of meat and clothing, was not always plentiful. Forest fires, severe storms and unusually harsh winters sometimes upset the delicate balance of nature leading to shortages and starvation. Hunting and fishing grounds were assigned and laws strictly controlled these activities in the various seasons of the year.

To the south of the Micmac lived the Abenaki, who were of Algonkin origin, controlling the land into the State of Maine. On the north shore of the St. Lawrence opposite the Gaspe the Montagnais ruled the territory as far east as Quebec City and the Naskapi up into Labrador.

In Newfoundland the Beothuk led a nomadic life taking the bounty of the sea in summer and moving to camps in the interior during the winter. Little is known of the Beothuk as the hostilities between them and the Eskimos of Labrador and the early Europeans led to their decline as a viable culture.

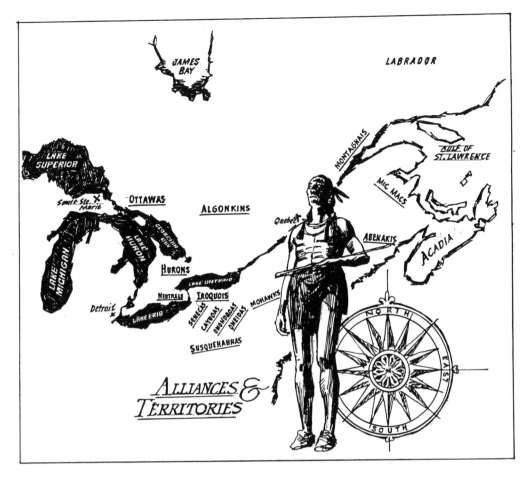

**Eastern
Canada's
First Nations
c. 1500 C.E.**

To the west of the Micmacs along the south shore of the St. Lawrence the Iroquois held sway at the time of Cartier's second voyage. The description of Hochelaga on the Island of Montréal suggests an Iroquois town and if so they occupied the north shore of the river as well although this would change before the coming of the French settlers.

The Iroquoian government was quite different from those of their neighbours. About 1400 A.D. the great Ho-de-no-sau-nee Confederacy of the Five Nations was forged between the Mohawks whose territory extended from the St. Lawrence well into New York State, the Oneida, who were their western neighbours, the Onondaga, the Cayuga and the Seneca. The territory of this Iroquois Confederacy stretched almost to the Niagara River.

The confederacy met at a grand council at Onondaga to decide matters of war and to settle disputes between the member tribes. They ratified treaties and approved any major wars to be fought by either all of the tribes or even one. For example, the Seneca could not mount a substantial raid or war without the consent of the council.

Here the Iroquois had a tradition that was unique among North American Indians. Although the women of the tribe did not serve on the council it was the matrons, the older women in the tribe, who nominated the members of the council. Not only did they nominate, but could impeach a member for misconduct. The matrons also controlled the food supply. If they disapproved of a planned raid or war they simply withheld food for the war party. Despite their power the chiefs did not force the issue. Thus a delicate balance was maintained within the tribes and the confederacy.

Among the Iroquois as well the lineage of a person was taken from his mother. Everyone belonged to a clan named for an animal, for example, the Turtle Clan or the Bear Clan etc. One was not allowed to marry into his or her own clan. When married the husband went to live in the longhouse of his bride. If he were of the Turtle Clan and his wife of the Bear Clan his children would be of the clan of his mother.

The Iroquois Confederacy was a powerful one as the Europeans discovered as they settled this vast land.

23

CANADA, A VILLAGE OF SMALL HUTS

Neere unto it, there is a village, whereof Donnacona is Lord, and there he keepeth his abode: it is called Stadacona, as goodly a plot of ground as possibly may be seene. Jacques Cartier, 1535

Although the English did not follow up on Cabot's voyages immediately an attempt at further exploration took place under the patronage of King Henry VIII in 1522. Like his father, he did not supply the funds for the venture, but made his royal wishes known to the merchants of London. Unlike their Bristol brothers the London merchants had no stomach for risk and adventure, but, they equipped two small ships named the *Samson* and the *Mary of Guildford* for an expedition. The *Samson* was lost at sea, but the *Mary of Guidford* made her landfall and made a reconnaissance of the American coast sailing south. Off Puerto Rico the Spanish greeted them with broadsides and the *Mary of Guildford* turned for home.

The dream of a passage to Cathay still haunted the mariners of Europe. One Gaspar Corté-Real of the Azores sailed from Lisbon, Portugal and was the first to penetrate Hudson Strait. He loaded the holds of his two ships with natives, which were sold as slaves on his return to Portugal.

Meanwhile the young King of France, Francis I, was anxious to establish a claim to a part of the new continent. In 1524 he engaged Giovanni de Verrazzano, a pirate who had been raiding the Spanish Main, to go and get him a piece of the pie. Verrazzano sailed from Dieppe in the *Dauphine* and made his landfall on the Carolina coast. He sailed north to Belle Isle between Newfoundland and Labrador noting the fine harbour where a great river spilled into the Atlantic (the Hudson) along the way.

He reported that the northern half of North America was rich and temperate and ripe for exploitation. Francis I was embroiled in a war in Italy, however, and Verrazzano was captured and hanged as a pirate. Francis himself was captured and taken to Spain as a prisoner so this adventure went for naught.

Francis was released from his captivity and was more determined than ever to stake his claim in the new world. This time he set his eye on the merchants and fishermen of St. Malo. Opposition to the thought of colonizing the new land was heavy in St. Malo. The fishermen sailed to the Grand Banks unencumbered by government regulations. Colonization meant bureaucrats, which meant taxes and duties.

However reluctantly, the merchants of St. Malo were determined to send their best on this mission and the best was an excellent navigator named Jacques Cartier. They outfitted two small caravels with a crew of 30 each and goods to trade with the mandarins of Cathay.

April 20, 1534 dawned chilly and overcast. The two caravels tugged impatiently at their cables as if anxious to quit the land. They had to wait however, while a solemn ceremony took place on the jetty. None other than Charles de Mouey, Sieur de la Milleraye, Vice Admiral of France and confidante of the king, had come to see the expedition off.

The reason for the elaborate ceremony was that King Francis, knowing the reluctance of the St. Malo merchants, wanted to insure that all would go according to plan. Each sailor, from the most experienced to the lowly cabin boy, sworn an oath before the Vice Admiral of all of France to serve, "Faithfully and truly the King and your commander."

Within twenty days of sailing Cartier made his landfall at Cape Bonavista, Newfoundland. Bonavista Bay was still clogged with ice, however, and Cartier was forced to seek shelter in a harbour a few leagues south. In gratitude for this sanctuary he named it St. Catherine's Harbour in honour of his wife.

After overhauling his ships he turned north again to the narrow strait between Newfoundland and Labrador that the fishermen who came to these waters called Belle Isle. When they arrived a violent storm was blowing from the west, which turned the fast flowing waters that sought the Atlantic into a maelstrom. No sailing vessel could make headway against such a force of nature. Cartier, convinced that this was the fabled Northwest Passage, anchored in what is now Kirpon Harbour to wait out the gale before striking into the heart of Cathay.

Cartier at the Strait of Belle Isle

The winds subsided on June 9th and Cartier turned the two caravels into the narrow strait soon emerging into open water again. He made Blanc Sablon on the Labrador coast describing those dangerous shoals as a bight offering no shelter. He also spoke of the many islands alive with tinkers, sea gulls and puffins. They quickly reached Brest Harbour where he went ashore to explore the surrounding area.

Cartier came back disillusioned. This was not the long sought Northwest Passage, but the mouth of a powerful river. Of the north shore he wrote, "I did not see a cartload of good earth. To be short I believe that this was the land that God allotted Cain."

Being the good pilot that he was he realized that he should find the south shore of this river and he turned south crossing the west coast of Newfoundland then turned due west. He was quickly rewarded with the discovery of the Magdalen Group of Islands. He continued on and charted the north shore of Prince Edward Island finally coming to the mainland entering

a wide bay he named the Baie de Chaleur, the name it carries to this day.

As Cartier rowed ashore fifty canoes filled with warriors, faces painted with white and red ochre came into view. They screeched and yelped threateningly and Cartier turned back toward the ships. The warriors dug in their paddles to intercept and soon surrounded the boats. At a signal from Cartier two of the cannon on board the ships fired. To the French sailors this was a mere bang and a puff of smoke, but to the Indians it must have been as if the every evil spirit in the world had been unleashed at that moment. They paddled away as fast as they could.

The Indians were braver than their initial response might seem and when they realized that no harm had come to them they renewed their menacing approach to the boats circling in an attack formation. This time Cartier took no chances. A volley from their muskets was too much for the warriors and they retreated. Cartier recorded in his journal, "They would no more follow us again."

Cartier turned north from here and soon discovered another large bay that he hoped was the breakthrough to the passage, but he soon discovered that he was wrong. Now convinced that this was the mainland he erected a thirty foot wooden cross with a shield nailed to it on which the fleur-de-Lis had been carved. At the top was inscribed: "Vive le Roy de France" long live the King.

A crowd of Indians had gathered to watch and soon had some idea that these strangers in their multicoloured clothes were claiming this land as their own. The Indians began to shout "Cassee Kouee!" the cry of the dreaded Iroquois meaning "Go away! Go away!"

After leaving this place they sailed north to Anticosti Island before pushing on a little further. Cartier knew then that they were on the fringes of a great, new continent. He went ashore at Anticosti and stood at the western tip of the island watching the fast flowing waters of the St. Lawrence. The passage narrowed here and he knew that he was truly at the mouth of a great river.

After consulting with his crew he set sail for home vowing to come again to this new land. The European phase of the history of Canada had begun in earnest.

*

When Cartier sailed back to St. Malo in August of 1534 he took with him two natives, Taignoagny and Damagaya, the sons of one of the chiefs. They willingly accepted his invitation to sail across the great ocean. We can only imagine how the great cities of France looked to the two Indians of Canada. Whatever their reaction they seemed to have adapted quite well to the situation. They quickly picked up a workable knowledge of French and were soon telling eager audiences of their native land.

One of the stories that caught the imagination of everyone, especially King Francis, was the story of the Kingdom of Saguenay. The two weaved a tale of fabulous wealth where gold could be mined in huge quantities. The natives there dressed in cloth as did the Europeans and wore precious stones around their necks. This Kingdom was located far up a mighty river, which flowed into an even greater river where a city of many wigwams called Hochelaga stood on an island. These were the stories that the king wished to hear. Francis, normally a very frugal monarch, decided to finance the next expedition himself.

On May 19, 1535 three ships, the *Grande Hermine* of 120 tons, the *Petite Hermine* of 60 tons and the pinnace *Ermillion* of 40 tons sailed from St. Malo. With them went the two natives and a distinguished company including Jean Guyon, Charles de la Pommeraye, Jean Poulet, and Claud de Pontbriant, a son of the Lord of Montréal and cup bearer to the Dauphin, all adventurers in search of fabled Cathay.

The *Grande Hermine* outsailed her consorts and arrived off Newfoundland on July 7th. After rounding the northern tip of the island she anchored at the chosen rendezvous, Blanc Sablon. The *Petite Hermine* and the *Ermillion* limbed into the anchorage on July 26th and after three days for repairs the three set sail into the gulf and headed west.

They sailed passed Anticosti and two days later sighted the twin peaks that marked the mouth of the Saguenay River. Cartier was awe struck by this rush of water, which came crashing into the St. Lawrence through the gorge that split those black cliffs in two. The two Indians must have told Cartier that this was the Saguenay, but he chose to push on rather than look for the fabled Kingdom of Saguenay. Taignoagny told him that to the west was Canada (meaning a village of small huts), which Cartier mistook for the name of the entire country. He was confident that he would find the route to Cathay and the treasures it promised if he sailed up the St. Lawrence.

As the *Grande Hermine* and her consorts made their way up the St. Lawrence the vast, silent continent began to unfold itself. Finally the ships came in sight of the most beautiful island that the crew had ever seen. Cartier called it the Ile de Bacchus because of the wild grapes that grew there. Eventually this place would be called Orleans. Natives were seen in the woods and they began to flee in a panic until they saw Taignoagny and Damagaya. This was the tribe to which they belonged. The year before they had been on a fishing expedition in the Gaspé when Cartier erected his cross and the two had sailed to France. Panic turned to joy at the reunion of the two brothers with their tribesmen and their father, Donnacona.

After a brief respite Cartier was determined to push

on to Hochelaga further up river instead of staying at Stadacona, the tribe's home village. It was a small settlement of wigwams laid out in a clearing along the river. Donnacona tried to dissuade Cartier from going further stating simply that it would not be wise. Taignoagny urged them not to go even producing three medicine men who made dire prophecies of the Frenchmen's fate should they proceed.

Leaving two of his ships behind, Cartier took fifty men in the *Ermillion* and headed up river. Nine days of easy sailing brought them to the Island of Montréal where they were greeted by a thousand natives who marveled at the these pale skinned strangers. Cartier left us a detailed description of Hochelaga, one which is hard to reconcile with what we have uncovered or not uncovered as the case may be. He wrote of a large community set in the midst of large, cleared fields at the base of a mountain that he christened Mount Royal. The city was round and "encompassed about with timber, with three courses of rampires, one within another, framed like sharp spikes." Inside this

palisade were about fifty houses, built of wood. Some were fifty paces long and fifteen wide all covered in bark. Each house had a centre court for building fires and the interiors were divided into several rooms. The problem is that there is no archeological evidence on the Island of Montréal for such a city.

Be that as it may, Cartier reported that their chief had confirmed the existence of the Kingdom of Saguenay and it lay along the Ottawa River. By means of gestures and pointing to the silver chain of Cartier's whistle and the dagger of copper gilt hanging from the belt of one of the sailors they assured them that these metals were to be found in abundance in the country along the Ottawa.

The natives warned Cartier that the land along the Ottawa was controlled by the Agojudas, a fierce and cruel people. They also explained that Canada extended far to the west and was enclosed by huge lakes guarded by high waterfalls. Here was a wilderness that could be settled by industrious people who could wrest a living from the land.

After a brief stay Cartier returned to Stadacona and found the crew left behind had not wasted their time. They had built a stockade on the banks of the Lairet a small tributary of the St. Charles River. It was fortified with cannon from the ships mounted to cover the approaches. Cartier added a moat and drawbridge to further strengthen their position. Splitting his crew between the fort and the ships Cartier settled in for the coming winter.

*

Cartier did not know what to expect with the onslaught of winter. He prepared as best he could. The ships were towed up the small stream and moored before the fort. The small company settled in to face whatever nature threw their way.

Snow was not unknown to these sailors of Brittany, but the cold and the blizzards of a Quebec winter must have been beyond their comprehension. The snow drifted up the walls as high as the sentry's lookout and, except for a narrow passageway to keep a line of communication with the ships, all attempts to clear the endlessly falling flakes was abandoned.

The Indians visited the fort daily at first, wading through the snow to trade. However, as the season progressed their visits became less frequent and their demeanor became as cool as the weather. In early December a mysterious disease struck the crew as well as some of the natives. Damagaya, one of the Indians that went to France the year before, was one of the natives infected. Cartier assumed that this pestilence had its origins with the natives and he forbad them coming to the fort. Cartier wrote: (This translation is from the work of Hakluyt writing in 1600,thus the odd spelling and archaic language) "In the moneth of December, wee understood that the pestilence was come among the people of Stadacona, in such sort, that before we knew it, according to their confession, there were dead above 50: where upon we charged them neither to come neere our fort, nor about our ships, or us. And albeit we had driven them from us, the said unkownen sicknes began to spread itselfe amongst us after the strangest sort that ever was eyther heard of or seene, insomuch as some did lose all their strength, and could not stand on their feete, then did their legges swel, their sinnowes shrinke as blacke as any cole. Others also had all their skins spotted with spots of blood of a purple coulour: then did it ascend up to their ankels, knees, thighs, shoulders, armes and necke: their mouth became stincking, their gummes so rotten, that all the flesh did fall off, even to the rootes of the teeth, which did also almost all fall out. With such infection did this sicknesse spread itselfe in our three ships ,that about the middle of February, of a hundreth and tenne persons that we were, there were not ten whole."

Having driven the natives from the area of the ships and fort their visits ceased altogether and Cartier increased his vigilance for fear that they might attack the ships and the fort. We now know that the crew was suffering from scurvy, a disease brought on by the lack of fresh food especially fruit and vegetables. The men began to die in great numbers and the toll reached fifty before a cure was found. Ironically it was the natives who discovered the remedy.

Cartier had remained healthy throughout the winter and to keep the extent of the problem among his men from the Indians he frequently walked out along the river with his healthy comrades. One day in March Cartier met Damagaya who was cured of the ailment and he inquired how he had cured himself. After some probing he gave him the recipe. The bark and needles of the white spruce were ground up and boiled and given to the patient. The remedy was tried with some reluctance, but within a few weeks all signs of scurvy disappeared from the crew.

With the approach of spring Donnacona and Taignoagny left Stadacona and visited some of the tribes to the south. These were probably the Iroquois from the Finger lakes district. They returned with a band of warriors and Cartier feared the worst.

The game of cat and mouse between the French and the Indians began. Cartier's scribe wrote: "How Donnacona came to Stadacona againe with a great number of people, and because he would not come to visit our captaine, fained to be sore sicke, which he did only to have the captaine come see him."

On the 21st of April Damagaya came to the shore across from the fort and announced that Donnacona would come the next day with deer meat and other gifts. A large number of warriors were observed in Stadacona and Cartier sent Jean Poulet into the town

with gifts for Donnacona who was in bed apparently ill. Poulet was escorted everywhere and was only allowed in certain areas, but he was able to confirm the presences of a the strange warriors in the town. Donnacona continued to make excuses for not coming to the fort throughout April.

Cartier finally determined to take hostages and sail for home at the first opportunity. On the 3rd of May the ice broke up in the St. Lawrence and a cross was erected in thanksgiving. Cartier invited Donnacona and the two interpreters to come for a feast aboard one of the ships. Anxious to determine the strength of the French they accepted. Ten Indians including Donnacona came on board and were immediately made prisoners. The following day Cartier set sail leaving the empty *Petite Hermine* at anchor and the Indians wondering about their chiefs. Donnacona was allowed on deck to shout reassurances to his people as the ships sailed out into the St. Lawrence.

On June 4th Newfoundland was sight and perhaps it is fitting to end this second voyage with Cartier's own words: "The Sonday(sic) following, being the fourth of June,... we had notice of the coast lying eastsoutheast, distant from the Newfoundland about two and twenty leagues:...we stayed till tewesday that we departed thence, sayling along that coast untill we came to Saint Peters Islands (St. Pierre & Miquelon). ...Whilst we were in the sayd Saint Peters Islands we met with many ships of France and Britaine (Britanny),... we went from that port, and with such good and prosperous weather we sailed along the sea, in such sorte, that upon the sixth of July 1536 we came to the Porte of S. Malo, by the grace of God, to whom we pray, here ending our navigation, that of his infinite mercy he will grant us his grace and favour, and the end bring us to the place of everlasting felicitie. Amen."

*

On reaching France with his hostages Jacques Cartier proceeded to Paris where he was granted an audience with the king, Francis I. With him went Donnacona, the chief, who had learned enough French to carry on an intelligent conversation. As had his two sons before him he wove a tale of the Kingdom of Saguenay, a land rich in gold. Francis, in his finery, appliqued and jeweled coat with a doublet trimmed with genet and chains of gold, was mesmerized by this king from across the sea in his buckskin leggings and skin shirt.

Francis was determined to push on with his exploration of the New World despite the objections of Charles, King of Spain, who claimed all of the newly discovered continent as his own.

Things looked extremely promising for the French efforts in North America, but, of course, politics intervened to dampen the whole affair. The plan was to send out colonists and artisans to cement any claims made in the King's name. Instead of leaving the enterprise in the hands of Cartier the king decided that someone of noble birth should lead the expedition. His choice was Jean François de le Roque, Sieur de Roberval of Picardy.

Roberval was neither a seaman nor an experienced leader. It soon became apparent that he was a poor choice for such an adventure.

Plans pushed ahead and Roberval was given the title, Lord of Norembega (Nova Scotia, southern New Brunswick and part of Maine), Viceroy and Lieutenant General in Canada, Hochelaga, Saguenay, Newfoundland, Belle Isle, Carpunt (the straits and islands between Labrador and Newfoundland), Labrador, the Great Bay (the Gulf of St. Lawrence), and Baccalaos (An early name for the entire northeastern part of North America. To this was added funds to equip an expedition. Jacques Cartier received the post of Captain General with the pronouncement of the king, "We are resolved to send him again to the lands of Canada and Hochelaga, which form the extremity of Asia towards the west."

Roberval was authorized to take from the prisons such felons as might serve a useful purpose in the enterprise. He began to gather his resources in a most leisurely manner and without regard to Cartier's wishes. Cartier had estimated a need for six ships of 100 tons burden and two barques of 50 tons each for the return. He requested provisions for two years with 120 sailors and 150 others to consist of all the trades required to set up a colony and mine and process the riches of Canada. Roberval came up with five ships and the reluctance of artisans to join the adventure cut back on the grandiose plans.

Early in May 1541 Cartier was ready to sail, but, Roberval was not. The king had made it clear that he would be displeased at any undue delay. Finally Roberval's contingent arrived, not the skilled artisans requested, but almost exclusively convicts who arrived in gangs chained together under armed guards. All was ready.

The Sieur de Roberval, however, was not ready to sail. He had supplies stored in ports all along the Norman coast. He was taking his time in assembling his part of the expedition. It was rumored that Roberval had no intention of sailing immediately for Canada, but instead had employed a notorious pirate, Pierre de Bidoux, and was going to do a little buccaneering on the way.

Cartier finally decided to wait no longer and on May 23 he set sail from St. Malo on his third voyage to Canada. After a stormy crossing he dropped anchor at Stadacona on August 23.

Cartier was greeted by the chief left in charge by Donnacona and he faced a delicate situation. All but one young girl of the ten prisoners taken to France were dead. What should he tell his host? He finally told him that Donnacona had died, which pleased the new chief as he was now confirmed in his post. The others, Cartier told him, were living in France and did not wish to return as they had married and were raising families. The chief accepted the explanation.

Despite the friendly welcome Cartier realized that an attempt to found a colony would be met with resistance by the natives. He immediately set to work to secure a base and the mouth of the Cap Rouge River was chosen as the site of the settlement. Cartier named it Charlesbourg Royal. Two forts were built and an acre and a half was cleared for cultivation.

While all this preparation continued a discovery up the Cap Rouge sent a stir of excitement through the colony. Iron flakes and gold were found in the sand along the banks. They mistook the quarts crystals for diamonds and they were sure that they had found the fabled Kingdom of Saguenay.

Before the onset of winter Cartier was determined to visit Hochelaga. He set out with a few of the company and arrived off the Island of Montréal to a less than enthusiastic welcome. His first visit in the eyes of the Indians was just that, a visit, but his return rightly signalled an intent to stay. He immediately set out for Cap Rouge without landing, but a party of Indians under the chief at Hochelaga proceeded him and Cartier was under no illusions that they were on their way to Stadacona to plan the destruction of the intruders.

Cartier hoped that Roberval had arrived at Cap Rouge but in this he was disappointed. He decided to send two ships back to France before the winter freeze with news of his discoveries. As the sails faded over the horizon the small band settled in for the winter.

As winter took hold the native population became increasingly hostile. Cartier knew that except for the forts they would attack and destroy the colony. Their old nemesis, scurvy made its appearance and the many of the convicts must have yearned for their prison cells.

In the meantime Roberval prepared for his delayed departure from France. He sailed from the port of La Rochelle on April 16, 1542. The crossing was long and arduous pulling into the harbour at St. John's, Newfoundland on June 8. They were amazed to find no fewer than seventeen fishing vessels from England, France and Portugal in the area. A few days later Jacques Cartier sailed into the harbour with his three ships and a much depleted crew.

Sparks flew the instant the two met. Roberval accused Cartier of deserting his post. Cartier accused Roberval of negligence in leaving him to winter with too few men and supplies surrounded by hostile Indians. Roberval ordered Cartier to return to Stadacona with him. Cartier refused stating that his men were so ill that he would not subject them to further suffering. In the middle of the night Cartier slipped anchor and sailed for France.

Roberval set out for Charlesbourg Royal and took possession of Cartier's forts. He expanded them and set in for the winter. Roberval proved a harsh disciplinarian and a poor administrator. He sat in judgment over the colony punishing malefactors for the pettiest of crimes. A man named Gailler was caught stealing and was promptly hanged. Men and women were sentenced to the lash for minor offences. One participant reported that six men were shot in a single day. Even the hostile natives of Stadacona were sympathetic to the plight of the intruders.

Spring brought the breakup of the ice on the St. Lawrence and Roberval gathered the remnants of his dispirited group and sailed for France ending the first attempt to colonize Canada.

THE FUR TRADE

"In truth, my brother, the beaver does everything to prefection. He makes for us kettles, axes, swords, knives and give us drink and food without the trouble of cultivating the ground." Indian hunter to a French trader, 1609

Before continuing our journey through Canada's Story we will take a look at the fur trade, arguably the single most driving force in the history of our country. The fur trade spurred the exploration of North America in general and Canada in particular. It dictated the relationship between Europeans and the Indians that inhabited the forests, plains and lakes from Acadia to the Pacific Ocean.

The fur trade in its turn was driven by one animal, an amphibious rodent, that once numbered above ten million in North America when Cabot first sighted the coast of Newfoundland. The beaver (Castor canadensis) became the most prized fur in the trade and was the standard by which the value of all others was judged.

Crestien Le Clercq described the beaver thus: "The Beaver is of the bigness of a water-spaniel. Its fur is chestnut, black, and rarely white, but always very soft and suitable for the making of hats." It seems that the further north one went, the darker the colour of the fur. Champlain wrote in regards the beaver in 1616: "As for the country south of this great river (*St. Lawrence*), it is very thickly populated, much more than on the north side . . . but, on the other hand, there is not so much profit and gain in the south from the trade in furs." The quality of the furs taken north of the St. Lawrence was considerably better due to the colder climate. Colour ranged from black in the north to a brown in the more temperate regions. In the Illinois territory the colours ran to almost yellow, the colour of straw. Young beavers tended to be darker in colour with a lighter undercoat and were the most valuable. As with all other animals the beaver's fur was much thinner and of poorer quality in the summer.

The fur of the beaver was of two kinds, the guard hairs, which were two inches long, and the under fur, about an inch thick. The Baron de Lahontan described this under fur as, "the finest down in the world." The fibres had numerous small barbs, which made it unusually suitable for the making of felt and felt hats.

The fur trade began as a subsidiary activity of the fishing fleets that worked the Grand Banks of Newfoundland. The demand for cod in Europe was enormous and the fishermen were in constant need of better ways to preserve their catch. Dried cod, rather than salted, became the most popular way to preserve the catch. This method necessitated the search for suitable harbours to land their catch for drying. As the various harbours were occupied more remote areas were explored bringing the ships in contact with more Indians.

Although limited in the early stages the fur trade began from the days of Cartier. In 1534 Cartier described a fleet of canoes in the Gulf of St. Lawrence, probably manned by Micmacs, who held up furs on sticks and motioned for the sailors to come ashore. Cartier wrote, "they sent on shore part of their people with some of their furs; and the two parties traded together. . . . They bartered all they had to such an extent that all went back naked without anything on them; and they made signs to us that they would return on the morrow with more furs."

The importance of the beaver in the trade at that time had not yet become apparent. Marc Lescarbot writing at the time of Champlain stated, "In the time of Jacques Cartier, beavers were held in no esteem; the hats made thereof are in use only since that time; although the discovery thereof is not new, for in the ancient privileges of the hat-makers of Paris, it is said that they are to make hats of fine beaver (which is the same animal); but whether for dearness or otherwise the use thereof had long since been left off."

The early trade was concerned with fancy furs that were valued for the beauty, lustre and warmth rather than their suitability for felting for hats.

In the latter part of the 16th century beaver hats came into fashion and demand in the Paris market skyrocketed and the fur trade came into its own. By this time the agriculturally inclined Iroquois had been driven from the St. Lawrence Valley by the hunters of the Algonkins, Montagnais and other tribes. Hunting was the livelihood of the tribes living in the lands drained by the Saguenay and Ottawa Rivers and they readily adopted their routine to satisfy the French appetite for beaver. Furthermore the hunting of beaver was not new to these northern people. Beaver was

used for clothing and it was this fur that was sought by the hat makers of Paris.

The treatment of the pelts were most important in the trade. The Indians took the pelts in their prime and the inner side scraped to loosen the guard hairs and then rubbed with marrow. The pelts were then trimmed into a rectangular shape with five to eight being sewn together with moose sinew to make a robe. This garment was worn with the fur next to the body. After fifteen months of constant wearing the guard hairs would fall out leaving the down fur. The pelts became well greased and pliable, ready for the hatters skills. These prime pelts, taken in the winter, were later classed as *castor gras d'hiver*. The length of time required to produce this *castor gras* forced the fur traders to move farther and farther into the interior to contact new tribes of Indians resulting in the rapid exploration and mapping of the continent.

Coupled with the French appetite for furs was the Indian demand for European goods. Kettles especially

made the Indian's life easier. Until the introduction of the iron kettle rocks had to be heated and dropped into clay pots to boil water for cooking. Clay was fragile and could not be put directly on the fire. Suddenly a long and laborious task was eliminated and the kettles transported without breaking.

The Indians were not passive players in this fledgling business. After an initial stage of accepting what was offered the Indians quickly became discerning consumers of European manufactured goods as we shall see in the weeks to come. Tribes along the St. Lawrence pushed inland to trade with the more remote tribes and jealously guarded what they considered their territory. Direct French intrusions were discouraged, sometimes forcibly.

The introduction of European goods, especially iron, caused a problem for the fur trade. The Indians were by nature conservationists and would always leave at least a pair of adults in a lodge to help keep the beaver supply coming. That, combined with the difficulty in breaking into a beaver lodge with their primitive tools of stone and bone, kept a balance between supply and maintaining a viable beaver population. Iron made the task of hunting very easy and in the quest for more European goods whole beaver colonies were destroyed. In a very short time the beavers of eastern Canada were all but wiped out. The French were particularly adept at the trade as they quickly became familiar with the Indian languages and customs. These French fur traders eventually became universally known as Canadians and the long road to nationhood began.

THE FATHER OF NEW FRANCE

"New France is not a kingdom but a new world, fair to perfection."- Samuel de Champlain, 1603

With the return of Roberval's contingent to France all ideas of establishing a French colony in the New World were shuffled to the back burner. Ships, including French, English, Portuguese and Spanish, made their runs to the Grand Banks of Newfoundland to reap the harvest of the sea. They used the many harbours and coves of Newfoundland for watering and shelter, but no attempt was made at a permanent presence. The fishing fleets discouraged settlement in an effort to keep the wheels of government and their inevitable regulations from the area.

Exploration continued, however, and in 1574 an Englishman, Martin Frobisher, received the support of Michael Lock, a member of the Moscovy Company, which traded with Asia through northern Russia, for an expedition. In 1576 Frobisher sailed with three ships from England in search of the elusive Northwest Passage. Only one ship reached Newfoundland, but Frobisher pushed on, sailing up the Labrador coast, crossing the entrance to Hudson Strait and coasting Baffin Island and eventually putting in at, what became known as, Frobisher Bay.

Frobisher took back a large rock with him to England, which an assayer claimed contained gold. Immediately, influential people including Queen Elizabeth herself subscribed to another expedition. The Cathay Company was formed, which was to have a monopoly "in all lands to the westward where Englishmen had not traded before." Frobisher lead voyages in 1577 and 1578, but no gold was found in the rocks taken from the shores of Frobisher Bay.

Sir Walter Raleigh's half brother Sir Humphrey Gilbert received a six year monopoly in 1578 and attempted to colonize the Canadian wilderness. His first effort ended when his fleet was dispersed by a storm and he was forced to return to England. He set out again in 1583. He took possession of Newfoundland in the name of Queen Elizabeth, but on his way back to England his ship, the *Squirrel,* was lost at sea just north of the Azores.

In 1584 another Englishman, John Davis, with the active support of Sir Walter Raleigh, obtained a charter to find the trade route to China. He set out in 1585 exploring the south coast of Greenland and crossed Davis Strait, but, the passage to the fabled western sea elluded him. He tried again in 1586 and 1587 but without success.

While the English sought the Northwest Passage the French began to renew their interest in Canada. French fishermen began to slowly forsake their fishing for the more lucrative trade in furs. They built crude huts along the shoreline of Anticosti Island and the Indians brought the fruits of their winter labours to trade. Bear and beaver were the major furs obtained.

In 1598 the Marquis de la Roche received a charter to colonize Canada. He ransacked the prisons and set sail in a small vessel and went forward to bring Christianity and civilization to the New World. At Sable Island he landed forty convicts and took his more trusted followers to explore the coastline in an effort to chose the site of the capital city of his new empire. His intent was to return and bring his colonists to the new site. A few days out from Sable Island a storm broke driving the ship far out into the Atlantic. De la Roche was forced to return to France. The marooned convicts watched for the sight of a sail in vain. It was to be five long years before another sail came. Only eleven of the forty were left alive.

With the close of the Religious Wars between the Catholics and Huguenots (Calvinists) with the Treaty of Vervins in 1598 France could once more look to external expansion. A bright young man of Saintonge on the banks of the Gironde River along the Bay of Biscay was to prove the driving force in France's American adventure.

Samuel de Champlain was born in 1567. His father was a sea captain and he trained his son to follow in his footsteps. Although a Catholic, Champlain was a follower of the great Huguenot leader, Henry of Navarre. In 1598 Henry recanted, became a Catholic and King Henry IV of France. With the close of hostilities Champlain sailed to Cadiz to deliver some Spanish mercenaries, taken prisoner during the war, home. It was in Cadiz that Champlain made a fateful

Samuel
de
Champlain

decision that was to alter the history of North America forever.

While in Cadiz Champlain accepted command of a Spanish vessel taking part in an expedition to the West Indies. He immediately saw the potential for a vast empire in the New World. He wrote a book about his adventures entitled *Bref Discours,* which brought him to the attention of the king. There were adventurous men at court who dreamed of finding a place for France in the vast territories beyond the western horizon. Champlain embraced the notion with enthusiasm and it was to consume the rest of his life.

Among the fishermen of France there also burned a desire to reap the wealth of Canada. In 1600 Henry granted a ten year monopoly in the fur trade to Pierre Chauvin of Honfleur and François, Sieur du Pontgravé of St. Malo provided they brought out fifty settlers each year. They chose Tadoussac at the mouth of the Saguenay for their colony. After trading with the Indians the two entrepreneurs returned to France

leaving the colonists to their own devices. That winter was particularly severe and when they returned the following spring only five men had survived and they had abandoned the colony and went to live among the Indians. These were the forerunners of the famous Coureur de Bois of the fur trade who adopted the Indian lifestyle. Again the dream of a French colony in the New World became a nightmare.

Still those at the court of Henry IV hatched plans to set up an empire in the New World. In 1603 the Governor of Dieppe, Aymar de Chastes, organized a company to try again to colonize Canada. Among the investors was Pontgravé of St. Malo and the man chosen to act as the official observer and historian was Samuel de Champlain.

Two ships sailed for Tadoussac and arrived without incident. While the ships lay at Tadoussac trading with the Indians Champlain assended the St. Lawrence by canoe as far as the Lachine Rapids. Everything had changed in the years since Cartier had been there. Of

36

Hochelaga there was no sign. The Iroquois, with their cultivated fields and palisaded towns were replaced by wandering bands of Algonkin hunters. From them he heard wonderous tales of the vast country of giant lakes that lay to the west. Champlain knew at that point that his life's work was here and the seed of a New France finally germinated. However, the problem of a permanent settlement loomed large as the difficulties at Tadoussac showed.

*

The failure of the colony at Tadoussac proved a great disappointment to Champlain who was more convinced than ever that a vast empire lay waiting for those with the courage and vision to seize it. In analyzing the problem the winter stood out as the culprit in the piece. Summers were moderate and crops grew well, so the winters had to be overcome if a permanent settlement was to succeed.

The eyes of the French turned from the St. Lawrence to the region known as La Cadie, which covered all of the territory from Cape Breton Island to the northern part of the State of Maine. The winters there were moderate in comparison to the valley of the St. Lawrence. The driving force behind this plan was Pierre du Guast, Sieur de Monts, gentleman in ordinary of the King's chamber, and governor of Pons. De Monts became Lieutenant Governor in Acadia with viceregal powers. The foundation of the enterprise was a monopoly in the fur trade, all previous patents and charters being unceremoniously voided. With monopoly in hand de Monts and Champlain began preparations for their grand adventure.

Part of the expedition set sail on April 7, 1604 with supply ships under the command of Pontgravé of St. Malo to follow in a few days. Immediately problems arose. De Monts was a Calvinist and had to promise that the Indians would be instructed only by Catholic priests although Calvinist ministers were allowed to accompany the expedition to minister to the Huguenots in the party. No sooner had they sailed then the priests and ministers began first to discuss points of faith, then to argue and then to fisticuffs. A story was related that after they had reached La Cadie a priest and minister happened to die at the same time and the crew buried them in a common grave to see if they would lie together in peace.

After a long and arduous voyage they reached a small bay where they found a fur trading vessel, which de Monts seized under his charter of monopoly. He named the bay in honour of the poor trader named Rossignol to help soothe his loss. Today it is called Liverpool Harbour.

They waited a month for Pontgravé in an adjacent harbour that de Monts called Port Mouton because a sheep had jumped overboard as they dropped anchor. Pontgravé finally arrived with the supplies and the spoils of four Basque fur traders he had captured enroute.

With supplies in hand de Monts sent Pontgravé to Tadoussac to trade with the Indians and he sailed south in search of his destiny. The expedition finally entered the Bay of Fundy, which de Monts named Baie Françoise. They explored the coast line of the bay marveling at the racing tides that mounted to sixty feet as it boiled and foamed its way to brake on the quick sands of Chignecto Bay. They sailed into the Annapolis Basin and noted the splendid harbour facilities. The Sieur de Poutrincourt was so impressed by it that he asked de Monts for a grant of it so that he could bring his family out to settle. De Monts agreed and transferred the title to him. Poutrincourt dubbed his new domain Port Royal.

Champlain busied himself exploring the surrounding countryside. He took soundings in the bay and charted the principal rivers and harbours.

For military reasons it was decided to establish the colony on an island in the mouth of the St. Croix River where their guns would command the entrance to Fundy. They were to live to regret their decision.

All began on a positive note. A large, high roofed house was built for de Monts, his servants and aides on one side of a square with another house on the opposite side to house Champlain and the Sieur d'Orville, who came along to watch his investment no doubt. The rest of the area was given over to barracks, shops and storerooms. As winter set in, however, the weakness of their position became abundantly clear. The island was swept by northwest winds most of the time and it was impossible to keep warm. They had neglected to put basements in the buildings so food froze and then spoiled. Under such conditions scurvy made an early appearance and by the time spring

**Settling
in
Acadia**

arrived thirty-five of the seventy-nine colonists had succumbed to the disease.

Loading what was left of their supplies and the frames of their homes on the ships, the survivors began a search for a new location. The choice fell on Annapolis Basin, Poutrincourt's Port Royal.

While de Monts pondered his next move Champlain sailed on the 18th of June in a fifteen ton bark to explore the regions to the south. With de Monts, several of the gentlemen of the expedition and twenty sailors he pocked into the coves and indents in the Maine coast. He reached Cape Cod, which Champlain named Cap Blanc because of the white sand there, and steered southward to Nausett Harbour, which he called Port Mallebarre.

At Port Mallebarre several Indians came aboard to trade and all went well until a number of sailors went ashore in search of fresh water. An Indian grabbed one of the kettles being used to gather water and when

the sailor gave chase he fell under a hail of arrows. The French in the boats fired their guns and Champlain's arquebuss exploded nearly killing him. Those Indians in the act of trading jumped overboard except for one who was bound hand and foot. He was released soon after as a gesture of goodwill.

With provisions running low the party turned back to St. Croix and the move to Port Royal. They quickly cleared the land and began preparations for a second winter in the New World.

While de Monts struggled to keep his new colony alive forces were at work in Paris to disrupt his plans. His enemies lobbied against his monopoly and a ship from France warned that something had to be done to thwart their ambitions. Reluctantly de Monts sailed for France leaving Pontgravé in command with Champlain and his hardy companions to experience another Canadian winter.

*

The location of Port Royal was chosen carefully

with the St. Croix experience in mind. They chose the north side of the Annapolis Basin where they would be protected from the north winds that had been so devastating the previous winter. In mid August the move was made.

Life in Port Royal settled into a routine as the summer of 1604 drew to a close. All planted gardens despite the advanced season and cultivated them in anticipation of the harvest. Even Champlain got into the spirit. He wrote: "I also, for the sake of occupying my time, made one, which was surrounded with ditches full of water . . . into which flowed three brooks of very fine running water, from which the greater part of our settlement was supplied. I made also a little sluice-way towards the shore, in order to draw off the water when I wished. This spot was entirely surrounded by meadows, where I constructed a summer-house, with some fine trees, as a resort for enjoying the fresh air. I made there, also, a little reservoir for holding salt-water fish, which we took out as we wanted them. I took especial pleasure in it and planted there some seeds which turned out well. But much work had to be laid out in preparation. We resorted often to this place as a pastime; and it seemed as if the little birds round took pleasure in it, for they gathered there in large numbers, warbling and chirping so pleasantly that I think I have never heard the like." They could look forward to some comforts when winter reared its ugly head once again.

When de Monts sailed for France to fight his political battles a few of the colonists whose ambitions had been satisfied sailed home, but the majority of them looked to the coming winter with a confidence that was unknown just a few months before.

As if to compensate the survivors for their harsh treatment the previous winter mother nature held her fury in abeyance as the fall season progressed. The winter spent on St. Croix saw the first snow in October, but snow did not arrive until December 20th at Port Royal. When winter did set in it was a mild and gentle affair that saw the colony prosper. Families spent the cold months snug in their new homes before the hearth as comfortable as one could expect to be in the wilderness that was Canada.

Their old nemesis, scurvy, showed up on schedule and some died though not as many as had succumbed the winter before. Part of this reduction was attributed to the Fir Beer that they concocted. The tenderest branches from a fir tree were boiled in a large kettle three or four times. After discarding the branches a little molasses was added along with wheat yeast. The mixture was poured into a barrel and the brewing process began. When the mixture stopped frothing and bubbling a cork was put in the barrel and after four days the brew was ready for drinking. Not only did it help against scurvy, but it was excellent in cases of the gout and other such ailments.

As the winter progressed Champlain sought ways to keep the spirits of the colony up. One of his ideas resulted in the founding of *L'ordre de Bon Temps* (The Order of Good Cheer). Each man in his turn was chief steward for the day and wore a collar around his neck. It was his job to fill the long refectory table in the Great Hall with foods and delicacies of every kind. Each steward tried to outdo the others. The incumbent went to great lengths to acquire fresh fish and game as well as some surprise to awe his patrons of the day. Thus the winter was passed with relish as the ingenuity of the colonists brought a variety of plain and exotic dishes to the fare of Port Royal.

Despite the mild winter 26 percent of the colonists died from disease and accident, a staggering number by modern standards, but below average for the colonial experiences of the 17th century. Two winters were passed by the fledgling colony in this fashion and things looked bright for the pioneers of L' Acadie.

In March of 1606 Pontgravé fitted out a barque of 18 tons to undertake "a voyage of discovery along the coast of Florida." Champlain sailed with him on the 16th, but the voyage was plagued with misfortune from the beginning. No sooner had they set sail than a storm drove them ashore on the Grand Manan. The damage was quickly repaired and they set out again. On reaching their former winter home at St. Croix contrary winds and fog forced them to wait eight days there. Before proceeding Pontgravé decided to return the short distance to Port Royal to "see in what condition our companions were whom we had left there sick." While there Pontgravé himself became ill, but soon set out again although far from well. Disaster immediately overtook them. They had just cleared the basin when the rushing tide swept them aground. Champlain wrote, "At the first blow of our boat upon the rocks the rudder broke, a part of the keel and three or four planks were smashed and some ribs stove in, which frightened us, for our barque filled immediately, and all that we could do was to wait until the sea fell, so that we might get ashore. . . . Our barque, all shattered as she was, went to pieces at the return of the tide. But we, most happy at having saved our lives, returned to our settlement with our poor savages; and we praised God for having rescued us from this shipwreck, from which we had not expected to escape so easily."

The expedition was abandoned and while they awaited word from home provisional arrangements were made to return the colonists to France should no ship arrive with news of the fate of de Monts' appeal for an extension of his patent. The plan was for Pontgravé to take his people to Cape Breton or Gaspé where they could catch a trading vessel back to France. When neither de Monts or Poutrincourt arrived by the middle of June a new barque was constructed to replace the one lost in April.

Eyes strained for the sight of a sail as June passed into July and when no word came the dejected colonists bid farewell to their new home and set sail. Two men were left to guard the stores and it appeared that another attempt to settle Canada was to a failure.

The barque reached Cape Sable on the 24th of July where sorrow turned into rejoicing; coasting along in a shallop was Ralleau, de Monts secretary, who told them that Poutrincourt was making for Port Royal with a 120 ton ship while he, Ralleau, kept close to shore in hopes of intercepting Pontgravé should he be abandoning the colony. Champlain wrote, "All this intelligence caused us to turn back; and we arrived at Port Royal on the 25th of the month, where we found the above mentioned vessel and Sieur de Poutrincourt, and were greatly delighted to see realized what we had given up in despair." Marc Lescarbot, added, "M. de Poutrincourt ordered a tun (a large cask) of wine to be set upon end, one of those which had been given him for his proper use, and gave leave to all comers to drink freely as long as it lasted, so that there were some who made gay dogs of themselves."

The following year disastrous news arrived from France. De Monts enemies had prevailed and his monopoly was revoked. Without the fur trade the viability of Port Royal was gone. On August 11, 1607 a grieving people boarded ships and sailed for France. Acadia was abandoned, but a core of settlers were determined to return to make a home in Canada.

*

With the abandonment of Acadia in 1607 it was a disappointed Sieur de Monts and Champlain who met in Paris later that year. At their meeting Champlain showed de Monts a map and plan for the establishment of a permanent colony on the St. Lawrence. To chance another attempt at establishing a colony in Canada was ill advised if not foolhardy. De Monts risked financial ruin if such an attempt should fail and Champlain was under no illusions as to the reactions of the Indians to a French colony there. De Monts appealed to the king directly and Louis IV offered no help beyond a one year extension of his patent and the lifting of the stipulation that colonists must be taken along and provided for. After the one year it was to be every man for himself. At this, ordinary men would have counted their losses and turned to other endeavors, but de Monts and Champlain were not ordinary men. They immediately set plans in motion to found a settlement at Quebec. With the backing of some of the earlier investors three ships were outfitted to sail from St. Malo bound for New France.

The Sieur du Pontgravé departed for Tadoussac on April 5, 1608 with one ship and two ships sailed eight days later, one headed for the St. Lawrence under Champlain while the other made for Acadia. In early June Champlain arrived at Tadoussac where he found the post under the control of Basque traders who were defying de Monts monopoly. They had fired on Pontgravé when he arrived killing one of his men and wounding himself and one other. Champlain found him very ill and the prospects of a fight for the post. Fortunately, on reflection, the Basques were sorry for their rash action and signed an agreement that they would not interfere with de Monts rights. Finally on June 30th Champlain set out for Quebec.

On July 3, 1608 Champlain dropped anchor at Orleans. He wrote in his journal, "From the Island of Orleans to Quebec the distance is a league (three nautical miles). I arrived there on the third of July, when I searched for a place suitable for our settlement, but I could find none more convenient or better than the point of Quebec, so called by the savages, which was covered with nut trees."

**Champlain
at
Quebec**

Champlain stood on the shore well satisfied with his choice and gazed up at the great rock that dominated the area. This he christened Mount du Gas in honour of his friend and patron, the Sieur de Monts.

Work on the colony began in earnest. Champlain sent a barque to Tadoussac for supplies and set the rest of his men to cutting down the trees and building shelters. While some sawed boards others dug cellars and trenches. When the work was done the new colony at Quebec boasted three frame houses of two stories with a three cornered courtyard with a watchtower in the centre. Around these stood a stout wooden wall, which reached the level of the first story, with a gallery with loop holes through which the defenders could fire their muskets in the case of an attack. Cannon protruded at intervals covering the approaches from the water and a moat covered three sides with the river taking care of the fourth.

The building completed, Champlain next encouraged his men to plant gardens that they might lay up stores for the coming winter. He led by example and marked out his own plot to the west of the fort. With axe and spade he laboured diligently in hopes of a bountiful harvest come fall.

It was while Champlain was busy supervising the preparations for the coming winter that Canada nearly lost one of its founders. A locksmith named Jean Duval hatched a plot to kill Champlain and turn the colony over to the Basques. With promises of riches beyond their dreams he managed to subvert four of the crew guarding the supplies aboard ship. Two plans were devised, one was to strangle him while he was unarmed and the second to raise an alarm at night and shoot him as he rushed to answer it. All was set and the date selected, but, Natel, one of the conspirators, had a change of heart and confessed to Testu, the pilot.

The traitors were seized and taken to Pontgravé at Tadoussac. Pontgravé returned them to Quebec where a courtmartial sentenced them to death. Three were reprieved and sent to France for their punishment

Champlain battles the Iroquois

while Duval, to quote Champlain, "was strangled and hung at Quebec, and his head was put on a pike, to be set in the most conspicuous place on our fort, that he might serve as an example to those who remained, leading them to deport themselves correctly in future, in the discharge of their duty; and that the Spaniards and Basques, of whom there were large numbers in the country, might not glory in the event."

Pontgravé set sail for France leaving the little company of twenty-nine to settle down to spend their first winter at Quebec. When it came, the winter of 1608-09 came with a vengeance. The meager vegetables that the gardens had provided were quickly eaten and most of the food consumed was that brought from France. They were able to supplement their diet with game from the forest and the St. Lawrence provided an abundance of eels, but the latter, if not properly cooked, resulted in dysentery, which often proved fatal. In February scurvy made its appearance. Jacques Cartier's remedy had been forgotten and Champlain watched helplessly as the disease took its

toll. When word came on June 5, 1609 that Pontgravé was back at Tadoussac Champlain wrote, "This intelligence gave me much satisfaction, as we entertained hopes of assistance from him. Out of the twenty-eight at first forming our company only eight remained, and half of these were ailing."

Such heavy losses would have discouraged most, but Champlain was more determined than ever to conquer this brave New World.

*

With the return of good weather and supplies from France Champlain was determined to consolidate his position in the New World. A letter from de Monts requesting him to return to France to brief him on the progress of the colony was put in off until the end of the shipping season so that he could pursue his goals.

About this time a chief of the Montagnais Indians was forming a war party to raid the territory of the Iroquois. Although Champlain was reluctant to participate in the battles of the local natives, a promise

42

had been made to them that the French would help their new neighbours against their enemies. He also saw an opportunity to explore the country and perhaps cement the French relationship with the Indians of the St. Lawrence Valley. Taking twenty men and leaving Pontgravé in command he set sail from Quebec on June 18, 1609.

At Eloi Island Champlain was met by 300 Huron and Algonkin warriors anxious to join the expedition against their ancient enemies. These warriors were led by two chiefs, Iroquet and Ochatequin who began a long harangue to the Indians gathered there. He urged them to follow Champlain against their enemies.

Champlain in his turn assured the chiefs of his support. He further assured them that he had come, not as a trader, but, as a soldier to fight beside his friends. Champlain's assurances pleased the gathered warriors and the Hurons and Algonkins promised to join the expedition, but they wanted to go to Quebec to see the houses of the French first. Anadabijou, chief of the Montagnais, made a long speech to his warriors praising the friendship of the King of France and the Frenchmen among them who would help them against their enemies. Thus the alliance forged in 1603 between the French and the Montagnais, Huron and Algonkin nations was ratified.

They finally left Quebec on June 28th. Accompanying Champlain and the Indian warriors were Claude Godet des Marets, La Routte, a pilot, and nine men. The French shallop (a heavy boat) sailed along the St. Lawrence followed by the canoes of the Indians to the Richelieu River and then proceeded south into the country of the Iroquois. The Indians had assured Champlain that the Richelieu was navigable as far as a great lake so you can imagine his chagrin when they encountered a waterfall with no means of moving the shallop past it. Despite this set back Champlain was determined to go on. He ordered all but two men to return to the mouth of the Richelieu while he continued on with the warriors in a canoe.

As the war party prepared to move up to the great lake the ranks of the warriors began to thin. Quarreling among the different tribes as well as the fact that there were now only three Frenchmen to accompany them into the territory of the vaunted Iroquois gave many pause to reflect on the foolhardiness of entering the lion's den. Portaging around the waterfall the expedition pushed on.

They entered the Grande Isle Channel and what unfolded before the eyes of the astonished Frenchmen was the largest inland lake they had ever seen. They marveled at this island studded expanse of water. Champlain dismissed as nonsense the claims of the Hurons that even larger lakes lay to the west. Champlain named this magnificent body of water after himself.

The party moved cautiously to Lake George, which Champlain named Lac St. Sacrament. On the 29th of July they sighted a cluster of canoes. They lay heavy in the water and the Hurons recognized them as elm bark canoes; only one tribe used them, the Iroquois.

This was unlike any Indian warfare known to this time. Usually surprise was the watchword of the day, moving quietly and attacking the enemy when he was off guard. The two groups approached each other openly challenging the other to battle with jeers and name calling across the tranquil waters of the lake. The Iroquois, for all their posturing, were not about to fight an open battle on the water. After haranguing the French and Indian party they made for the shore where their knowledge of woodcraft would serve them well.

As evening fell the night air was filled with the war songs of the Iroquois as they danced around their fires, voices full of confidence for the coming battle. The Hurons and their allies were equally as defiant returning jeer for jeer, seeing their own war songs, however, they did not venture ashore. Lashing their canoes together, they spent the night on the water.

As dawn broke the Frenchmen donned their breastplates, polished so that they would gleam in the sun. Champlain put on casque with a plume as a show of leadership and ordered his men to load their weapons and check their swords and daggers. It was arranged that the French would go ashore in separate canoes and stay spread among the warriors to give more effect to the firing of their guns. To surprise the overconfident Iroquois the French hid themselves under robes in the canoes and stayed behind the line of battle in the initial stages.

The Iroquois came out for battle taunting their

Champlain among the Hurons

enemies. Champlain estimated about two hundred warriors faced his small party of sixty. He was amazed at their appearance, tall and physically magnificent, they were superior in every respect to his own Indian allies. They proclaimed their victory in advance, their voice high with confidence. Three chiefs with the white plumes of their office on their heads led the way waving their stone hatchets, calling on their enemies to fight if they dared.

At this point the ranks of the allies parted and Champlain strode forward slowly into the gap. The Iroquois fell silent. Who were these white gods with their shining breasts? Champlain knew that the pause was only momentary and soon the Iroquois would get over their initial shock. He also knew that his allies could not sustain a charge from their enemies who outnumbered them significantly. The difference between life and death now hung in the balance. Everything depended on the steadiness of his hand and the sureness of his aim.

He had loaded his arquebus with four bullets and now took aim at the three chiefs who stood in a group at the front of their warriors. The explosion shattered the morning air and when the smoke cleared the three chiefs lay on the ground two of them killed instantly.

Although dismayed by this turn of events and unable to understand the nature of this new weapon, the Iroquois responded with a hail of arrows. At that juncture one of Champlain's men stepped forward and fired into the ranks of the Iroquois. This was too much for them and they fled with the allies in hot pursuit. Many Iroquois were killed and about twelve captured.

The Hurons and their allies had won a great victory and the celebrations began. One of the prisoners was chosen for torture. He was lashed to a stake and told to sing his death song. Before he was finished the wood piled at his feet was set ablaze and the most cruel torture began.

Champlain finally demanded that the torture be

44

stopped, but the excited warriors refused until they realized that Champlain friendship might be at stake. They allowed him to put a bullet through the young warrior's heart ending his ordeal.

Thus ended Champlain's first encounter with the Iroquois. Many French Canadians were to rue that fateful day of the summer of 1609.

*

On returning to Quebec from his foray against the Iroquois Champlain made preparations to sail back to France to report to de Monts. He set out for Tadoussac to confer with Pontgravé as to the best course of action to ensure the survival of the new colony. They decided that they should both go to Paris to help de Monts persuade the king to extend the fur trade monopoly; without it Quebec was not financially viable. Before departing they returned to Quebec to appoint someone to command in their absence, someone who could hold the small company together through the harsh realities of a Canadian winter. The task fell to Pierre de Chauvin.

Chauvin, who Champlain called Captain Pierre, was born at Dieppe of a prominent Norman family. Before joining Champlain on his New World adventure he had resided at Honfleur. Champlain gave the young nobleman detailed instructions taking every precaution to avoid the disaster of the previous winter. On September 1, 1609 Champlain sailed from Quebec and made a silent vow to return as he watched Cape Diamond fade in the distance. Champlain had accomplished much in one year. Aside from his participation in the battle against the Iroquois he had explored parts of the Saguenay River by canoe with his Montagnais allies, explored the St. Lawrence as far as the Richelieu River and cemented the French hold on Tadoussac and the fur trade that it controlled. His support of the raid on the Iroquois confirmed the alliance with the Montagnais and their chief, Anadabijou as well as the Hurons and Algonkins under Iroquet and Ochateguin. With careful observation of customs and manners he now had a grasp on the best ways to promote trade with the indigenous peoples of Canada.

After a stop at Tadoussac he sailed for France on September 5th with the knowledge that the fledgling community of Quebec was ready as it could be for its second winter in the wilds of the St. Lawrence Valley.

On dropping anchor in France Champlain and Pontgravé immediately proceeded to Fontainebleu, where they were ushered into the presence of King Henry and de Monts. Champlain presented the king with a girdle made from the quills of a porcupine, two finches the colour of a carnation and the head of a fish caught in Lake Champlain, which had a long snout and two or three rows of sharp teeth, probably a pike.

Champlain reported on his activities and discoveries in the New World and it was obvious that the king was impressed, but would he extend de Monts monopoly? It seemed reasonable under the circumstances to do so, however protests from the merchants of Brittany and Normandy left the Canadian fur trade open to all.

De Monts again refused to give up the dream even in the face of shrinking resources. He went to Rouen to consult with his two associates, Collier and Legendre on their next course of action. Despite the setbacks and potential for financial ruin, de Monts convinced them to finance another season. Two vessels were outfitted, one with supplies for Quebec and the other for the fur trade under the command of Pontgravé. Champlain, much to his dismay, was informed that his services were no longer required, however, de Monts gave him permission to accompany the expedition if he chose.

After some delays the ships sailed from Honfleur on April 8, 1610 arriving at Tadoussac on April 26th, one of the fastest voyages on record to that date. There Champlain was met by a young nobleman, Jean Godet, Sieur du Parc, who had wintered at Quebec with Chauvin. The news from that quarter could not have been better. All the settlers had survived the winter with their old nemesis scurvy making but a brief appearance. The liberal use of fresh meat seems to have been a factor in the well being of the colony. Champlain set out for Quebec arriving to a heroes welcome a few days late.

The Indians were anxious to see Champlain return. They were gathering a war party and wished Champlain to lead them again. Sixty Montagnais came to Quebec with a number of Basques. Such was their respect for Champlain that they presented themselves saying, "Here are numerous Basques and Mistigoches who say they will go to war with us.

What do you think of it? Do they speak the truth?" Champlain replied, "No, I know very well what they really mean; they say this only to get possession of your commodities." The Indians said, "You have spoken the truth. They are women and want to make war only upon our beavers."

Champlain led another successful foray against the Iroquois in which a hundred warriors were massacred by his Huron and Algonkin allies. In this battle Champlain was wounded in the neck by an arrow, but he recovered quickly and headed back for Quebec. In appreciation the Hurons promised to show him the three rivers and the great lake that resembled a sea, the end of which could not be seen. Champlain made a mental note of the promise and started back for Quebec.

In the meantime des Marets arrived from France with disturbing news. The king, Henry IV, had been assassinated. Champlain left du Parc in command at Quebec and sailed for France on August 8th arriving at Honfleur on September 27th. He rushed to see de Monts and his worsed fears were confirmed. De Monts' influence at court had evaporated with the king's death. The future of the colony at Quebec was once more in jeopardy.

De Monts had little to show for the second year of his Quebec colony. With wide open trade a number of vessels appeared in the St. Lawrence to barter for beaver. Pelts that were obtained for two knives now cost twenty as the traders bid for furs. Champlain knew that some order had to be brought to the trade if anyone was to benefit from it.

While Champlain struggled to establish Quebec, Port Royal in Acadia sat deserted, but not forgotten. Poutrincourt, his title confirmed by the king was determined to return to his beloved Acadia. In February, 1610 he descended the Seine and Aube Rivers to Dieppe with a boat load of provisions for Port Royal. There a ship waited and on February 26th he sailed for New France full of anticipation and hope. After a stormy crossing he entered the sheltered anchorage at Port Royal anxious to see what the passage of time had wrought. To Poutrincourt's surprise the buildings still stood with but minor damage to the roofs. Even the furniture was undisturbed in the rooms. The old chief, Membertou was there to greet them. As he had promised, the French were back in Acadia. The struggle to survive as a colony and as a people was just beginning for them.

THE VOYAGES OF HENRY HUDSON

"Into the ice we put for safety. Some of our men fell sick. I will not say it was for fear, though I saw small sign of other grief."- Henry Hudson, 1610

While Champlain nursed the fledgling colony at Quebec and Poutrincourt was busy reestablishing the settlement at Port Royal in Acadia the English were still contemplating the Northern Passage to Cathay. In April of 1607 Henry Hudson made the first attempt to reach Asia by the northern route. In the employ of the Muscovy Company he sailed in the *Hopewell* up the east coast of Great Britain and attempted to circumvent Greenland but was stopped by ice just north of Spitzbergen in the Barent Sea. After exploring Spitzbergen he headed home discovering Bear Island and Jan Mayen Island on route.

In 1608 Hudson made another attempt, this time by the Russian route via the Kara Sea. Again ice blocked all attempts to get through and he turned west in search of the Northwest Passage, however, his crew forced him to return to England.

English interest in a northern route waned with the failure of Hudson's second attempt, but he was determined to press on. The Dutch East India Company, much larger and wealthier than the Muscovy Company, was interested in a shorter route to the east. Hudson persuaded them to sign a contract with him to search for the Northeast Passage. Note that Hudson was instructed to seek a Northeast Passage and his employers were very specific knowing his tendency to turn his ships westward.

On March 25, 1609 Hudson sailed from Amsterdam in the service of the Dutch East India Company. His ship was the *Half Moon*, built in Holland for the company. He dutifully sailed for the Kara Sea and Siberia. After clearing North Cape they entered the White Sea where they encountered severe storm activity forcing them back. Hudson abandoned his attempt and instead of returning to Holland he broke his contract and sailed west.

On the 3rd of July Hudson found French fishermen busy on the Grand Banks and on the 9th he made a landfall at Sable Bank, Nova Scotia. After speaking with a French fishing vessel he turned south, crossed the Gulf of Maine and sighted Cape Cod on the 3rd of

August. He sailed south as far as Cape Hatteras, South Carolina before turning north to the Chesapeake and on to the Hudson River, which he sailed up as far as present day Albany. On October 5th he sailed for home landing at Dartmouth in Devonshire at the end of the month.

Hudson wanted to persuade his Dutch backers to finance another attempt at finding the Northwest Passage the following year, but English authorities refused permission for him to sail to Amsterdam. He had to be content with reporting to the Dutch counsel in London. England squelched any plans for a Dutch attempt at the passage by forbidding Hudson's participation.

Despite all the setbacks and failures Hudson made one more attempt at getting backing for another expedition. This time an independent group of merchant adventurers led by Sir Thomas Smythe agreed to pay the bill. Hudson took command of the Bark *Discovery* and made plans to sail. With what he had learned on his previous voyages Hudson knew that the passage did not lay along the eastern seaboard of the New World, but lay somewhere north of 60 degrees latitude through one of the many straits in northern Canada. Armed with his convictions and his charts he set sail on the 17th of April 1610.

Hudson sailed up the east coast of Great Britain as he had done before and made landfall at Iceland on the 11th of May. After a brief stay he set out westward again sighting the east coast of Greenland on the 4th of June in the land of the midnight sun. Hudson described it in his journal:
"June 4 We saw Groneland (sic) over the ice perfectly, and tonight the sun went down due north and rose in the north northeast.
June 5 Still encumbered with much ice which hung upon the coast of Groneland,. . .

On the 9th of June Hudson was off Frobisher Bay from where he sailed southwestward for six days when he sighted the land that John Davis had named Desolation. He then turned Northwestward until he

**Henry Hudson
set adrift on
Hudson Bay**

reached Latitude 60 degrees 42 minutes on the 20th making note of ice and a strong current flowing from east southeast to west northwest. In early July Hudson entered Ungava Bay where the first signs of trouble showed itself among the crew. After being trapped in ice some demanded to go home while others sided with Hudson. Once free from the ice pack things settled down and the voyage continued.

On leaving Ungava they sailed through Hudson Strait arriving off Mansel Island on the 3rd of August. Hudson explored the east coast of the bay, which bears his name reaching as far south as James Bay. Here trouble brewed among the crew again and Hudson replaced the mate, Robert Juet and the boatswain naming Robert Bylot to the former and William Wilson to the latter positions.

Despite the problems with his crew and the low state of supplies Hudson decided to winter in the bay. On the 10th of November he landed at today's Rupert House and made preparations for the winter. The ship was hauled up on shore and a shelters built. Ducks and geese were hunted to supplement their diet and all settled in for the winter. As if an omen of things to come the gunner, John Williams, died shortly after landing.

By the end of November the shoreline of the Hudson Bay was frozen and the rigors of an Arctic winter made itself felt. The fowl taken by hunting parties soon were eaten and scurvy began to make its appearance adding to the misery afforded by the cold and snow. In desperation the men began haunting the woods and valleys in search of anything eatable. One such expedition inadvertently discovered a treatment for scurvy. Thomas Woodhouse, a scientist , brought back a tree bud that was full of a turpentine-like substance, which the surgeon mixed up as a drink. It immediately relieved the pain caused by the disease.

With spring and the breakup of the ice Hudson and his crew were ready to leave their lair. In preparation Hudson had his men set nets for fish to restore their larder for the future. Meanwhile Indians appeared and one of their number traded two beaver and two deerskins to Hudson promising to return. A few days later some Indians were observed setting the woods on fire. Hudson set out in the shallop to make contact, but, although they continued to set fires in sight of his party he was unable to meet with them.

On the 18th of June the *Discovery* set sail and had gone but a short distance when the majority of the crew mutinied. The deposed mate, Robert Juet, and one of Hudson's proteges, Henry Greene, were the ringleaders. Hudson, his son John and six men were set adrift in the shallop with little supplies. Hudson was never heard of again. In 1612 Captain Thomas Button sailed on a rescue mission, but no trace was found.

The crew sailed for home but not without incident. On landing for supplies a fight broke out with local Indians and five including Henry Greene were killed. Robert Juet died before reaching England.

Hudson did not perish in vain. England laid claim to the great bay and set the stage for the great French/English rivalry that lasted 150 years.

THE WINTER OF JENS MUNCK

"As I have now no more hope of life in this world, I request for the sake of God if any Christians should happen to come

While France and England vied for supremacy in the North America the Danes had ambitions to follow the great Norse legends and in search of Vinland and Markland. King Christian IV himself supervised the preparations for the Viking return to America.

The choice of commander fell on a young officer of the Danish Navy, Jens Munck. Munck came by his position in the Danish Navy in a very roundabout way. He was of noble birth, but his father was imprisoned for misuse of public funds, where he committed suicide. Destitute and without influence the twelve year old Munck shipped out as a common sailor to seek his fortune. He happened to be aboard a Dutch vessel that was attacked and destroyed by a French man-o-war off Bahia. Munck and six others survived making their way ashore where the Munck worked as a shoemaker's helper and as an apprentice painter.

When he was eighteen years old some Dutch ships arrived in Bahia without a license to trade. Munck overheard the authorities talking about seizing the ships. He swam out to the Dutch to warn them and they upped anchor with their benefactor on board.

Within five years of his return to Europe Munck was sailing the northern seas to Iceland and Russia. In his late twenties he joined the Danish Navy making a name as a skilled navigator. To him fell the task of founding a new Viking empire in the New World.

Two ships were outfitted for the enterprise, the Unicorn, a frigate with a crew of forty-eight and the Lamprey, a sloop manned by sixteen sailors. On Sunday May 16, 1619 Munck sailed for Hudson Bay with the intention of establishing a Danish colony in the vast reaches of the Arctic ice fields. Many of Munck's crew were pressed into service and the voyage had an ominous beginning. One of the reluctant sailors jumped overboard rather than face the prospects of a voyage to the northern seas and another died of natural causes a few days later. This was a harbinger of things to come for the expedition.

Despite the deaths of two crewmen so early in the

voyage Munck made excellent time sighting Greenland in twenty days. To take advantage of the southerly currents he lashed his two ships together and ran into a field of soft slob ice, which would protect the ships from the larger ice flows and bergs. He then let the current take them down toward the straits that would take him into the bay. Though it was summer, sleet plagued them as they slowly drifted south leaving long icicles hanging from the rigging. The heat of the day set everything dripping, as the sun dipped below the horizon the cycle was repeated.

In early July the two ships were finally separated from their lashings and began to worm their way into Hudson Strait through the drift ice. At times the vessels had to be towed by throwing grapnels onto the ice and the crew pulling them along. The men had to be constantly on guard with ice poles to keep the heavier flows from crushing the hulls. Munck anchored off Baffin Island to give the exhausted men some rest. Here they suffered their first loss in the bay, Andrew Staffreanger, a seaman, died and was buried on Baffin Island.

In late July, in the middle of the night, ice suddenly swept in on the two ships and men were tumbled from their berths by the thundering of ice against hull. The floors in the cabin were sprung and when the crew rushed on deck they were greeted by the sight of ice piled higher than the yardarm. The Lamprey's keel was gashed from stem to stern and no sooner was that repaired than the rudder of the Unicorn was carried away. Precious time was lost making repairs.

Munck was six weeks in traversing the strait and finally in the first week of September he sailed into Hudson Bay. Munck immediately began his search for a suitable location for his colony. He sailed down the western shore where a great sleet storm separated the two vessels. Munck spotted a small creek through hurricane driven sleet and skillfully maneuvered the Unicorn into it. He found himself in a land locked lagoon that was to become Churchill, Manitoba. The storm raged on for four days and the crew waded ashore at ebb tide to light signal fires to guide the

Lamprey in. Finally on September 9th a small sail was sighted and the tiny sloop slipped into the sheltered harbour and safety.

Munck moved his ships further up the harbour and prepared to winter in the bay. he built an ice boom around the ships and had huge stone fireplaces built on the decks of the ships and every scrap of clothing was issued to the crew. Used to the damp, temperate climate of Denmark, the descent of the harsh Arctic winter with its dry, bitter cold left the Danes helplessly paralyzed. They didn't know how to cope with such conditions. They had no furs and only the open fireplaces on deck for warmth. Red hot shot was put in pans to try to bring some heat to their miserable berths. They could do nothing but huddle about the fires piling more wood to drive the killing cold away.

Perhaps we can let Munck himself tell the story. The following are excerpts from his journal:

October 15: Last night, ice drift lifted the ship out of the dock. At next low water I had the space filled with clay and sand.

October 30: Ice everywhere covers river. There is such a heavy fall of snow, it is impossible for the men to go into open country without snowshoes.

November 27: All the glass bottles broken to pieces by the frost.

December 12: One of my surgeons died and his corpse had to remain unburied for two days because the frost was so terrible no one dared go on shore.

January 21: Thirteen of us down with sickness.

February 17: Twenty persons have died.

April 1st: Died, my nephew, Eric Munck, and was buried in the same grave as my second mate. Not one of us is well enough to fetch water and fuel. Have begun to breakup small boats for fuel. It is with difficulty that I can get coffins made.

May 6: Died John Watson, my English mate. The bodies of the dead lie uncovered because none of us has strength to bury them.

Munck finally took to his bed in June with the corpse of the cook's boy on the floor. Below decks lay three more corpses and three more on deck. Only Munck and two others were still alive and the two had gone ashore, but had not the strength to get back.

51

Munck lay for four days without food and penned a note asking for a Christian burial should he be found.

The stench became so bad in the ship that Munck finally dragged himself on deck and was surprised to see two men on shore. They dragged themselves over the flats and helped Munck to shore where they barely had the strength to kindle a fire to drive off the wolves. To satisfy their hunger they began to eat the green shoots beginning to sprout in the Arctic spring. They ate weeds that they could reach. This turned out to be their salvation for it was scurvy that wiped out Munck's crew and the green plants were the cure.

By the 18th of June the three survivors were able to walk out to the ships. Munck sank the *Unicorn* to keep it safe until he could return for it and the three sailed away in the tiny *Lamprey* arriving home without further incident.

Munck never returned to the bay because of wars in Europe that occupied the Danish Crown. He died in 1628. As for the *Unicorn,* Eskimos found the ship at low tide and while plundering the cargo put some of it over fires to dry. A keg of gun powder ignited blowing the plunderers and the ship to oblivion.

QUEBEC TAKES ROOT

"Where I searched for a place suitable for our settlement, but I could find none more convenient or better situated than the point of Quebec, so called by the savages, which was covered with nut trees."- Samuel de Champlain

While Henry Hudson explored the wilds of the bay that bears his name the fledgling colony of Quebec continued to establish deep roots in the virgin soil of Canada. As the twenty odd men prepared to spend the winter of 1610-11 in the wilderness Champlain continued the struggle in France to save his colony after the assassination of the king. The new Monarch, Louis XIII, listened to the pleas of de Monts and Champlain but declined to intervene in the question of the fur trade monopoly so important to the well being of the enterprise. Despite the setbacks Champlain continued to lobby for his beloved Quebec.

In the middle of all this Champlain, a 40 year old bachelor, contemplated marriage for the first time. The choice of a bride was an unlikely one. Champlain was a devout Roman Catholic and the chosen bride was a Calvinist and only twelve years old. Her name was Hélène Boullé. The marriage settlement was signed on December 27th 1610 at Paris in front of the family and friends of the betrothed.

In the agreement Nicholas Boullé agreed to pay a dowry of 6000 livres cash the day preceding the wedding and Champlain agreed to make his future wife the sole beneficiary of his estates and wealth upon his death. Boullé sent Champlain 4500 livres two days later with the rest to follow shortly thereafter.

The betrothal took place in the church of St. Germain L'Auxerrois on Wednesday, December the 29th and the following day the marriage was celebrated in the same church. Because Helene was not of age, she returned to her parents home for two years as stipulated in the contract.

His personal life now settled Champlain went to work on de Monts to finance another season in New France. Although the financial future was bleak, he pointed out that the expenses would be small. A few barrels of biscuits, pease and cider would be enough to sustain the small nucleus of men manning the colony. De Monts agreed and Champlain sailed on March 1, 1611.

The passage was a rough one and when they approached the Grand Banks of Newfoundland they fell among a great number of icebergs. The expedition was in danger of being crushed and the cold made it difficult to navigate the ships around the mountains of ice that sailed resolutely southward. They finally came in sight of Newfoundland where they met a ship carrying Beincourt, son of Poutrincourt, who was headed for Port Royal, but had lost his way. Champlain set him in the right direction and continued his journey arriving at Tadoussac on May 13, 1611.

To Champlain's dismay the entire country was still covered in snow and he sailed at once for Quebec, fearing the worst. Would he find a deserted settlement with only the buildings to show where there was once a thriving community? To his great joy and relief a very healthy du Parc and company greeted him on his arrival. Game had been plentiful all winter and scurvy had failed to make its customary appearance to the satisfaction of all concerned.

Champlain's joy at what he found at Quebec was tempered by the chaos in the fur trade. Reports of fabulous wealth to be had for the taking brought boat loads of adventurers with no idea of what they were doing. Most sailed away disgusted after a few days their only accomplishment being the driving up of the price of the furs. The only ones who would make a profit in 1611 would be the Indians.

Undeterred Champlain set sail for the upper reaches of the St. Lawrence exploring the country as he went and seeking a place to establish yet another settlement. He described his findings in his journal: "But in all that I saw I found no place more favourable than a little spot to which barques and shallops can easily ascend with the help of a strong wind, or by taking a winding course, in consequence of the strong current. But above this place, which we named *La Place Royale*, at the distance of a league from Mount Royal, there are a great many little rocks and shoals which are very dangerous.. . . After a careful examination, we found this place one of the finest on this river. I accordingly gave orders to cut down and clear up the woods in the Place Royale, so as to level it and prepare it for building."

Building homes in the wilderness

The men set to work constructing a fortification for their new enterprise as well as a store house and dwellings. The wall built was 1.2 metres thick, 1.2 metres high and 9 metres long. Champlain set it up on a rise 3.5 metres high to protect it from the spring floods. He named the Island Ste. Helene, in honour of his wife. The seeds of the great City of Montréal were planted.

On the 13th of June two hundred Hurons arrived at Sault St. Louis, named for a young man who had drowned in the rapids a few days before. These warriors were commanded by Ochateguin, Iroquet, and Tregouaroti. The latter was a brother to Savignon, a young Huron that Champlain had taken back to France with him the previous year. They told Champlain of a large sea that they had seen at a great distance from their village.

On the 18th of July Champlain departed for Quebec where he prepared to sail back to France. He planted some rose bushes in his garden and inspected the bumper crop of maize, squash, and beans that the rich summer sun was promising. It was a bumper crop that he would not enjoy. On the 20th of July he loaded some oak timbers on board his ship and sailed home. He arrived at La Rochelle on the 16th of September to find de Monts running the city of Pons in Saintonge, his fortunes at a low ebb and the future of New France very much in doubt.

THE ABORIGINAL CIVILIZATIONS

The Iroquois Confederacy was established sometime in the 15th century ending years of intertribal warfare. The league of Five Nations had their symbolic council fire burning at Onondaga, which was the sign of the covenant between the tribes.

With the establishment of the colony on Ile St. Helene Champlain was ready to push his efforts to explore the interior and see the great inland sea described by the Hurons. But he first set his sights on the great river that the Indians called Kichesippi and Champlain dubbed La Grande Riviere des Algoumequins. Today we call it the Ottawa River.

Before following Champlain up the Ottawa I feel that it is important that we meet the Indians that lived there and in the lands to the west. We have already been introduced to them, but not on their home turf. First, a look at where the occupation of the Ottawa Valley began.

The first substantial human occupation of the Ottawa Valley occurred after 4000 B.C. with the introduction of the Laurentian Culture. Important Laurentian sites have been found at Morrison Island and Allumette Island in the Ottawa River dating back to 3300 B.C.

There is evidence that the Algonkin and their Algonkian relatives were not descended from this culture, but from another known as the Shield Archaic Culture. These people migrated down from the Keewatin District of the Northwest Territories about 2500 B.C. They settled in the Canadian Shield and were dependent on Caribou and other game animals for their subsistence. This culture originated the use of the birch bark canoe for which the Algonkins became famous. About 700 B.C. the Shield Archaic Culture was replaced by the Laurel Culture, which saw the beginnings of the use of pottery and the ushering in of the Woodlands Period. There appears to be a direct link between this culture and the Indians living on the Ottawa at the time of the first European contact.

Archeological evidence found on Morrison Island suggests that the Algonkins have lived in the area for 1,000 years. They were hunter/gatherers who participated in the extensive trade network that crisscrossed the North American Continent. They traded birch bark canoes, meat, and furs to their allies,

the Hurons, for items from the south such as gourds, maize, and shells. We know that in 1534 the Iroquois controlled the St. Lawrence Valley and were enemies of the tribes further north. However, by the time of Champlain, the Algonkins had a firm grip on the Ottawa Valley and lands to the north and had driven the Iroquois into upper New York State and Vermont and had at least nominal control of the St. Lawrence west of Trois Riviere.

There were several bands living along the Ottawa. One of the more prominent was led by a chief called Besouat and they werecalled the Kichesippirini or the People of the Great River. They were headquartered on a small island between two rapids on the upper Ottawa near Pembroke, Ontario. The island is today's Morrison Island. The Weskarini called the area around the Petit Nation River, which empties into the Ottawa at Papineauville Quebec, their home.The band led by Iroquet called itself the Ouescharini or the People of the Fish Totem. Many smaller bands were dispersed throughout the area.

The Algonkins nearest neighbours were to the north. The Ojibwa and the Cree hunted in the area of James and Hudson Bay relying on the Algonkins for trade goods from the south.

To the east the Algonkins' powerful ally in their perennial wars with the Iroquois, the Hurons, dwelled in and around the country bordering Georgian Bay. Despite being related to the Iroquois, the Hurons were of Iroquoian stock, they were bitter enemies of the Five Nations.

This rivalry created one of the most historically fascinating situations in Canadian history. An extensive trade network embraced most of North America before the European conquest. In order to facilitate trade in an uncertain military climate where warring parties might come into contact with each other, a neutral site where safety was guaranteed was required. The Iroquoian tribe living in the Niagara Peninsula was the facilitators of this zone or Port of

The Iroquois Confederacy

Trade between the Iroquois and the Hurons.

This Port of Trade provided the Neutrals, so named by the French, with military security, protection for the traders, facilities for storage and agreement on the relative value of goods. The Neutrals were the middlemen in a complex trading network that functioned for two hundred years before the coming of the Europeans.

The Neutrals occupied territory that was on the border of two ecological zones. To the north the Hurons controlled the agricultural region of the southeast shore of Georgian Bay. They carried on trade with the Algonkins trading corn, nets, and tobacco for furs, birch bark canoes, dried fish, and meat. These in turn were traded to the Neutrals for gourds for oil, Raccoon skin robes from the Eries and shells from the southeast coast of the U.S. that passed from the Susquehannocks through the Iroquois to the Neutrals. Strombus, a large conch shell from the Gulf of Mexico was a regular trade item at Niagara.

This was the situation among the tribes of central Canada on the eve of Champlain's journey to the land of the Algonkins. The balance of power was to be forever altered by the European involvement in the affairs of the aboriginal peoples.

AUTHOR'S NOTE: The spelling of the name Algonkin has long been rendered Algonquin in Canadian history books. It appears that Algonkin is correct and will be used throughout Canada's Story.

*

As the French prepared to expand the fur trade westward they came to realize what a dangerous enemy they had made in the Iroquois. Their raiding parties ranged deep into Canadian territory along the St. Lawrence and Ottawa Rivers. Many of the tribes in the north refused to come down to trade or took circuitous routes to reach Trois Rivière or Quebec in order to avoid the Iroquois Warriors.

The Iroquois were the most advanced people of the first nations in North America. Their system of

56

government was even more sophisticated than that of the Europeans who regarded them as savages.

The Hodenosaunee or Iroquois Confederacy was established sometime in the 15th century and ended years of intertribal warfare. The League of Five Nations was made up of the Mohawk, Onondaga, Oneida, Cayuga and Seneca nations. It was a complicated alliance with a political system consisting of the a series of checks and balances. The symbolic council fire burned in Onondaga and was the sign of the covenant between the tribes. The council met at Onondaga on a regular basis or when something important was to be discussed. No major war or raid could be undertaken by a member tribe without the prior consent of the council. The Confederacy was also responsible for the security of the five territories of the tribes. If an enemy attacked one he attacked all.

The council also could direct a tribe to go to war on behalf of the confederacy. In 1712 the Cayugas made war on the Delawares and defeated them. The confederacy adopted them to act as a buffer between the them and the Cherokees. The Delaware were not allowed to go to war unless called upon to do so by the Iroquois.

The social and political structure of the confederacy was a delicate web of clan loyalties and interdependence. The family unit was too weak to face the rigors of survival on its own, therefore the larger unit, the clan, bound together several families who shared the labour and the resources to their mutual benefit. The clan shared a longhouse in a village that consisted of a number of clans. Clan names were taken from the animal kingdom. Among the Seneca, for example, the eight clans were Wolf, Bear, Beaver, Turtle, Hawk, Snipe, Deer, and Heron.

More surprising than their form of government is the place of women in the Iroquoian society. It was forbidden for anyone to marry within his or her clan avoiding the problems of intermarriage with close relatives. Clan lineage was taken from the female side, thus, the man always went to live in the longhouse of his bride.

It was the women who controlled the economic resources of the tribe. They assigned the work for the clan and subsequently the village. Contrary to the popular myth of the women doing all the heavy work, it was the men who got the most strenuous jobs to do. When a new field was required it was the men who chopped down the trees and cleared the land. The women did the planting, tending the crops, and grinding of the grain into flour. Food preparation and preservation was also the job of the women.

The men were responsible for another important source of food for the community, hunting and fishing. Much of the men's energy was spent laying up meat and fish for the winter.

Although the men ruled as chiefs and sat on the council, it was the women, or more precisely the matrons, who nominated the council elders and could impeach a member if necessary. They were consulted on matters of war and alliances with tribes outside the confederacy. The matrons also controlled the food supply and distribution was at their discretion. They had the power to withhold food from the council or even war parties thus affecting decisions made by them. If a chief mounted a war party that the matrons disapproved of they simply refused to issue rations for the raid. No food, no raid and the women vetoed unpopular wars much as modern parliaments do by withholding funds.

The confederacy was also a key player in the vast transcontinental trade that saw goods flow from the southern United States, through the Niagara Peninsula, to the north and vice versa. The Iroquois traded shells and agricultural produce for birch bark canoes and furs. With the coming of the Europeans this north-south trade became less important as the Iroquois turned to the east to obtain guns and European goods from the Dutch and English. It was this trade that made the Iroquois such a formidable opponent for the French settlers.

As we shall see the battle between the Iroquois and the French Canadians in the St. Lawrence Valley was to be a long and bitter one.

CHAMPLAIN & THE NORTHERN SEA

"I discovered a river flowing northward; I descended this river, and reached the shores of the sea."-Nicolas de Vigau, 1612

In the winter of 1611 Champlain and de Monts struggled to keep the Quebec colony alive. With the failure of de Monts to get help from the king, Louis XIII, he unhappily informed Champlain that he would have to abandon the enterprise.

Champlain was now on his own with resources too slender to support a colony in the early stages of development. Despite this setback Champlain was determined to continue, not just because of the years of work that he had put into it, but because he was sure, that with time, the project had every chance of succeeding with accompanying glory to both himself personally and to France. To succeed he knew he needed someone with power at the court of Louis XIII.

Champlain drew up a statement of facts and presented them to Maréchal de Brissac, President Jeannin, whom he knew was very interested in the happenings in New France. Jeannin immediately went to work and arranged the patronage of Charles de Bourbon, Comte de Soissons, then governor of Dauphine and Normandy. He promised to act on Champlain's behalf and the king granted de Soissons control of the settlement. He in turn made Champlain his lieutenant. Shortly thereafter the good comte died and the king committed the project to Monseigneur Le Prince de Condé, who retained Champlain as his lieutenant.

While in France he met a young man named Nicholas du Vignau, who claimed to have seen the northern sea where there was the wreck of an English ship. He told Champlain that the Algonkin River (Ottawa) flowed into a lake that emptied into it. The journey, he assured him, could be made from Sault St. Louis in seventeen days.

After arranging passage for du Vignau with a merchant of La Rochelle, Champlain sailed with Pontgravé on March 6, 1613 arriving at Pointe aux Vaches near Tadoussac on the 24th of April. The Indians came on board looking for Champlain fearing that he had stayed in France. One old man approached him and examined the scar on his ear caused by the arrow wound that he received in a battle with the Iroquois. On satisfying himself that it was indeed Champlain, he shouted with joy and was reported to have said, "Your people await you in Tadoussac."

On reaching Tadoussac Champlain found the Indians there on the verge of starvation. Dropping supplies he hurried on to Quebec anxious to see how the colony had faired in his absence. He reached there on May 7th and to his relief all was well with everyone enjoying good health. It had been a particularly mild winter, which had left the St. Lawrence open throughout.

On the 13th Champlain headed up river for the Island of Montréal and the Sault St. Louis, which he reached in eight days. There he met with several Algonkins who were no longer going down to trade because of bad treatment and his long absence from the country. They feared that he was not coming back. Champlain decided to visit his Algonkin allies.

He set out from Ile Ste. Hélène on May 27th, 1613 with a party of four Frenchmen including du Vignau and an Indian guide. They entered Lac St. Louis and then into country new to Champlain. Lac des Deux Montagnes, he named Lac de Soissons and he saw the Ottawa and its tributaries, the Gatineau River, the Rideau and Chaudière Falls. They pushed on to Lac des Chats passed the Madawaska River, Muskrat Lake and the many islands of the Ottawa.

As they approached one of the bigger islands a large group of Indians stood waving excitedly. On the beach to greet Champlain was his old friend Tessouat, chief of the Kichesippirini.

The island that the Kichesippirini called home was Morrison Island strategically situated between two rapids, which afforded them protection while giving them control of that part of the river. They exacted tolls from any who passed through much like the robber barons of the Rhine in Germany.

The following day the Algonkins threw a *tabagie* in honour of Champlain. The feast included corn broth, a stew made from meat and fish, charbroiled

venison and fish, and what Champlain described as "beautiful, clear water". When the feast was over all but the elders withdrew. They filled their pipes and each offered his to Champlain in turn.

Through his interpreter Champlain explained that the only reason for coming was "only to assure them of my affection and of my desire to aid them in their wars." He then explained that he wished to go on to the Nipissirini in order to invite them to go on the warpath as well.

Champlain failed to tell them of his main purpose, that of finding the Northern Sea and then on to the Orient. Tessouat was too shrewd not to see the great disadvantage in having the French make direct contact with his western neighbours. His role as middleman in the trade for European goods would be gone. The Kichesippirini were on the horns of a dilemma. They needed French help against the Iroquois, but were reluctant to give up the tolls collected from the Western Indians going to the St. Lawrence to trade.

Tessouat tried to persuade Champlain not to go

further. He described the Nipissirini as "wicked sorcerers, people of the small spirit, cowardly and useless in war".

Next came one of the most interesting exchanges in early Canadian history. Champlain pointed out that young de Vignau had been to the country of the Nipissirini without trouble. Tessouat addressed de Vignau by name in Algonkin saying, "Nicholas, is it true that you were among the Nebicerini?" "Yes," he said in the Algonkin language, "I was there." "you are a downright liar," replied Tessouat, "you know well that you slept at my side every night, with my children, where you arose every morning; if you were among the people mentioned, it was while sleeping. How could you have been as bold as to lead your chief to believe lies, and so wicked as to be willing to expose his life to so many dangers? You are a worthless fellow and ought to be put to death, more cruelly than we do our enemies."

De Vignau confessed to Champlain that he lied and had fabricated his story in order to get a free passage back to Canada. The Algonkins told Champlain,

59

"Give him to us, and we promise that he shall not lie anymore."

Champlain abandoned his plans to go further that year and promising Tessouat that he would return the following year, he set out for the St. Lawrence on June 10th. On the 17th they arrived at Sault St. Louis where they were greeted by Captain L'Ange, one of Champlain's officers, with the news that a merchant named Maisonneuve of St. Malo had arrived with a warrant from de Conde to trade. Champlain decided to return to France at the first opportunity and availed himself of Maisonneuve's hospitality for the voyage. The future of New France looked bright indeed.

THE FIRST SHOTS FIRED

Captain Samuel Argall's raid on the Acadian colony signaled a long struggle for dominance in North America.

While the French colonies at Acadia and Quebec were taking firm root on Canadian soil, the growing ambitions of the English to gain a foothold in the new world pointed to friction between the two powers in North America. As each laid claim to vast areas of unexplored country it was inevitable that there would be overlapping jurisdictions.

Like the French, the first attempts at colonization proved a failure. In 1584 a colony was founded on Roanoke Island off the coast of Virginia by Sir Walter Raleigh who named the entire area Virginia in honour of Queen Elizabeth. The territory covered everything from the Spanish settlements to the south to Newfoundland in the north. In 1586 supply ships found the colony deserted. the weary settlers had accepted an offer of passage back to England from Sir Francis Drake.

In 1587 Governor John White arrived at Roanoke with one hundred men , seventeen women and several children to reestablish a colony there. White returned to England promising to bring supplies back the following year. A naval war with Spain prevented his sailing back until 1591 at which time he found a deserted ruin with no sign of the colonists, including his daughter. Their fate has been a point of speculation to this day.

In 1606 the first permanent settlement at Jamestown, Virginia was founded. Unlike the French experience in Canada the Indians were hostile from the beginning and attacked the settlement at every chance. By the winter of 1612, despite these hardships, the colony took hold and the Governor, Sir Thomas Dale, turned his attention to securing the remainder of the lands claimed by England.

In the spring of 1613 Captain Samuel Argall sailed among the islands off the coast of Maine to fish for cod. Encountering some Indians he discovered the presence of some Jesuit missionaries close by. He assured them that he was a friend of the priests and one of the Indians took him to the spot where they were camped. Argall immediately opened fire on the vessels at anchor and killed or captured most of the

French there. He landed without opposition and found the camp deserted, the remaining French having fled to the safety of the woods. He found trunks belonging to the expedition's commander, La Saussaye and, removing the royal letters and commissions, carefully relocking the trunks. The following day he received the surrender of La Saussaye with courtesy and respect listening to his explanation of his royal letters and commissions and assured him that he would respect the lawful charge of the King of France. La Saussaye was ordered to produce the documents, which, of course, he was unable to do as Argall had them in his possession. Argall flew into a rage and accused the French of being in English territory illegally. He loaded them aboard his ship as prisoners and sailed for Jamestown.

Shortly after sailing Argall cast fifteen of his prisoners including La Saussaye and the Jesuit Massé adrift in an open boat. They were able to make it back to the islands where their pilot, who had not surrendered, took charge and after a perilous trip eastward fell in with some French trading vessels that gave them passage to St. Malo.

Fourteen other prisoners, including the Jesuit, Father Biard, were carried back to Jamestown to face Governor Dale. Argall spoke to the prisoners of the kindness of the governor and his love for the French. He assured them that their lives were safe and they would be treated with courtesy in Jamestown.

On landing the truth of the matter soon came to light. The volatile Dale ordered the gallows built and the prisoners hung for having the impudence to occupy the territory of King James I. Argall tried to reason with Dale by saying that he had guaranteed the French their lives, however, the governor was determined to have his executions. Finally Argall produced the stolen letters and commissions and Dale relented. He was determined, however, to rid the North American coast of the French intruders and ordered Argall to destroy the Acadian settlements.

Argall's first fell on Mount Desert where he destroyed La Saussaye's unfinished defences and cut

Samuel Argall burns Port Royal

down the cross planted there. They next crossed to St. Croix Island where they captured a quantity of salt and razed the remnants of de Monts' buildings. Having completed their work there they crossed the Bay of Fundy to Port Royal. They found the little settlement empty.

Beincourt was away with some of his men visiting one of the local Indian villages while the rest of the colonists were in the fields some distance away bringing in the harvest. The English immediately began to carry off or slaughter the animals in the nearby fields. After ransacking the building, plundering even the bolts and locks on the doors, they put the entire settlement to the torch.

As the dreams of the Acadians went up in smoke the raiders moved up river by boat to where the harvest was being gathered. The reapers fled to a wooded ridge when the English came into view. After burning the crops the raiders returned to their ship.

Biencourt, having seen the smoke from Port Royal

rushed home in time to see the English re-embark. Hopelessly outnumbered he tried to lure Argall into an ambush, but, this failed. He asked for an interview under a flag of truce where he asked for supplies to take them through the winter. Argall declined and with the French settlement at Acadia effectively eliminated, or so he thought, he sailed for Virginia on the 13th of November.

The Acadians struggled through the winter, living off the land and the generosity of their Indian neighbours. With the coming of Spring the undaunted Acadians began to rebuild their shattered colony.

Captain Samuel Argall's raid on the Acadian colony was the beginning of a long struggle for dominance in North America that was to last for 150 years, even during periods of peace between Britain and France. Despite this, the Acadians persevered and their contribution to Canadian history can be seen to this day.

ÉTIENNE BRÛLÉ: THE FORGOTTEN HERO

He was never happier than when he had a paddle in his hands propelling his canoe into unknown country.

One of the most neglected names in Canadian history is that of Étienne Brûlé. He came out to Canada as a servant to Champlain and was present at the founding of Quebec. He adopted to life in the Canadian wilderness like a native son, spending his winters with the Indians learning their customs and language. He was never happier than when he had a paddle in his hands propelling his canoe into the unknown country that was to be Canada.

Brûlé quickly went from servant to Champlain's interpreter in his dealings with the Algonkins and the Hurons. He blazed the trail for the fur traders seeking beaver and the missionaries who followed up on their heels in their quest to convert the Indians to Christianity.

It is important to remember that it took hardships and sacrifices to travel among the lakes and rivers of Canada in the early 17th century. This was not exactly a vacation. Brûlé left no written records of his journeys, but, a Recollect missionary left us an indication of what a journey was like. Father Joseph le Caron wrote to a friend: "It would be hard to tell you how tired I was with paddling all day, with all my strength, among the Indians; wading the rivers a hundred times and more, through the mud and over the sharp rocks that cut my feet; carrying the canoe and luggage through the woods to avoid the rapids and frightful cataracts; half starved all the while, for we had nothing to eat but a little *sagamite*, a sort of porridge of water and pounded maize, of which they gave us a very small allowance every morning and night."

Among the most trying of ordeals for the Europeans was the flies and mosquitoes that attacked them relentlessly. Another Recollect, Gabriel Sagard wrote: "If I had not kept my face wrapped in a cloth, I am almost sure they would have blinded me, so pestiferous and poisonous are the bites of these little demons. They make one look like a leper, hideous to the sight. I confess that this is the worst martyrdom I suffered in this country; hunger, thirst, weariness, and fever are nothing to it. These little beasts not only persecute you all day, but at night they get into your eyes and mouth, crawl under your clothes, or stick their long stings through them, and make such a noise that it distracts your attention, and prevents you from saying your prayers."

Étienne Brûlé very quickly adopted the Indian way of life. He dressed like an Indian, his hair unkempt, and he became, for all intense and purposes, one of them. He took a number of Indian wives, discarding them at will as he moved through the country. His good friend Father Sagard wrote sadly that Brûlé was "much addicted to women."

Brûlé quickly outstripped his employer and the missionaries. He was the first to ascend the Ottawa River and move up the Mattawa River to Lake Nipissing. He followed the French River establishing the route to Huron country. He visited Georgian Bay and Lake Simcoe. He descended the Humber River and was the first to view the future site of the City of Toronto. He crossed Lake Ontario, skirted Iroquois country, probably through the Niagara Peninsula, and reached the upper waters of the Susquehanna River in Pennsylvania where he came in contact with the Carantouan Indians of that region. He descended the Susquehanna and visited the northern tip of Chesapeake Bay.

On one of his return journeys from the Susquehanna Brûlé's party was surprised by a war party of Iroquois. Everyone scattered and ran for their lives and Brûlé found himself safe, but alone in the forest. After three days he was famished and decided to take his chances with the Iroquois. Finding an Indian trail he followed it until he came across three Indians in the distance carrying fish. He called to them in the Huron language throwing his weapons down in a show of friendship. The three took out their pipes and smoke with him before leading him to their village where they gave him food.

Now the situation became dangerous for Brûlé. "Are you not one of those Frenchmen, the men of iron, who make war on us?"

He answered that he was of a nation better than the French, and good friends of the Iroquois. His captors scoffed at such a story and had him tied to a stake. They began the ritual torture by tearing out his beard by the handfuls, and burning him with firebrands. Brûlé, a good Catholic, had an *Agneus Dei* around his

THE PORTAGE

neck and one of the torturers asked what it was, thrusting out his hand to take it. Brûlé, thinking quickly, said, "If you touch it you and all your race will die."

The Indian persisted. It was a hot, sultry day and Brule spotted a gathering thunder head. He pointed to the inky blackness as a sign that his God was angry. The clouds obliged him with several peeling claps of thunder. The superstitious Iroquois fled in terror. Their chief released him from the stake and had his wounds tended. There was not a feast or event that he was not invited to after his show of power.

After a brief period of captivity he was released into the territory of the Neutrals and spent some time in the Niagara Peninsula before pushing on to the west. When he did not return to Quebec Champlain assumed that he was dead.

Brûlé's first move after his release was to hook up with some Huron warriors and head west. He led a party passed Michilimackinac and into Lake Superior. Many believe that he was also the first European to see Lake Michigan. If this is true he was the first to see all the Great Lakes.

Étienne Brûlé's name should have gone down in Canadian history as a tireless traveler and forerunner of those great explorers that came after him, but, in the end he is remembered as a traitor who guided the English up the St. Lawrence to capture Quebec in 1629.

He met his end at the hands of his friends, the Hurons. In 1632 he was murdered in one of their villages near present day Penetanguishene.

THE MISSIONARIES

"The harvest is plentiful, and the labourers few."-Father Paul Le Jeune S.J. 1634

While the fur trade was the most important reason behind the French interest in Canada there was a secondary enterprise, which captured the imagination of Champlain. Being a devout Christian, Champlain feared for the souls of his new "heathen" allies and very early he brought out missionaries to preach the gospel to the Indians. In 1614 three Recollets, a branch of the Franciscan Order, came out to Canada with him. Fr. Joseph Le Caron immediately headed into the interior with the Hurons and wintered near Lake Simcoe with them to learn their language. He remained with them for two years amid great hardship returning to Trois Riviere on the 20th of May 1616. His main purpose in returning was to seek some help in the work he had undertaken. He was unable to return to Huronia until 1623 accompanied by Fr. Nicholas Viel and a lay brother, Gabriel Sagard. The Hurons welcomed the missionaries and built them a small chapel in their village after which Fr. Le Caron returned to Quebec leaving Fr. Viel to learn the language and minister to the Hurons. After acquiring a fair knowledge of the language Fr. Viel began instructing the Hurons in the Christian faith.

In 1625 the Recollets had a number of missions in New France including those in New Brunswick and Nova Scotia. There were missions at Quebec, Tadoussac, Trois Rivière, among the Nipissing and those already mentioned among the Hurons. The priests in Canada were anxious to expand their work, but there was a shortage of Recollets available to come to the New World. The new Viceroy of New France, Duc de Ventadour, at the request of the Recollets, invited the Jesuits to send out missionaries to Canada.

On the 19th of June 1625 three Jesuits, Frs. Enemond Massé, Charles Lalemant and Jean de Brébeuf, accompanied by the Recollet Joseph de la Roche de Daillon, arrived at Quebec. Their first impression of the colony was not a good one. Champlain was away in France and Emery de Caen said that he had no instructions from the viceroy to allow them to enter the colony. Furthermore, there was no room for them in the fort and due to a slanderous communique that proceeded them, no colonist would take them in. They saw no choice but to return home on the same vessel that brought them.

Suddenly a boat approached their ship manned by some Recollets in their distinctive, coarse, grey robes, with the knotted cord of their order around their waists and their peaked hoods hanging about their shoulders. They greeted the Jesuits with open arms and an offer to share their quarters along the St. Charles River. The Jesuits gladly accepted and upon landing knelt and kiss the ground of New France.

The Jesuits were indeed disappointed in what they saw in Quebec. Seventeen years after its founding it still had fewer than 100 permanent residents. Little if any attempts had been made at large scale farming and the colony was totally dependent on France for their every need. When not out gathering furs the traders lounged about the trading posts or lived among the Indians where they lived a life of drunkeness and debauchery despite the efforts of Champlain to curtail these vices.

The Jesuits, with the exception of Brébeuf, spent the winter of 1625-26 at the Recollet Monastery on the St. Charles. Brébeuf, anxious to study the Indians in their homes, joined a group of Montagnais hunters and accompanied them to their winter hunting grounds. He learned the Montagnais dialect and more importantly that boldness, courage and perseverance were qualities much admired by the Indians. He returned to his companions none the worse for wear and eager to begin his work.

In July of 1626, while Lalemant established the Jesuits at Quebec, Brébeuf, in company with a new arrival, Fr. de Noue and Joseph de la Roche, headed for the Huron country. They set out for Trois Rivière where they were greeted by a large number of Algonkins and Hurons. The missionaries made friends with the Indians there and prepared to continue their journey. While there, news was received by a runner of the Recollet, Fr. Nicholas Viel who was on his way to Quebec. His Indian guides had decided to shoot the rapids at Riviere des Prairie and Fr. Viel's canoe overturned and he and a young Huron convert named Ahaustic were drowned.

**Preaching
the
Gospel**

The next day the long journey to Huronia began in earnest. Brébeuf, a giant of a man, immediately impressed the Indians with his strength and endurance. He match them stroke for stroke with the paddle and carried his share of the load on portages without showing any sign of fatigue.

The journey was beset with danger. The Iroquois were raiding the Hurons and the French, even in the vicinity of Quebec itself. They paddled up the Ottawa, up the Mattawa, across the portage to Lake Nipissing, and down the French River. They arrived at Penetanguishene Bay at a village called Otouacha. They then trekked two kilometers to Toanche where they found Viel's cabin still intact. The three began the arduous task of mastering the Huron language before beginning to instruct the Indians in the Christian faith.

La Roche spent a short time among the Hurons before being summoned back to Quebec and de Noue,

unable to master the Huron language and suffering ill health left the country in the spring of 1627 leaving Brébeuf alone to carry on.

Although he was greatly admired by the Hurons, who affectionately called him Echon, he had little success in converting them to Christianity in those early days. They told him, " Echon, You want us to love the Iroquois, to take only one wife and love her for all time; you say that we must not eat the flesh of our enemies, and ask us to give up our medicine feasts and many other things. We tell you, you are asking something we cannot do, unless your God will change us from what we are."

In 1628 Brébeuf was recalled to Quebec and arrived to the rumours of a large English fleet on its way to the St. Lawrence. Brébeuf was anxious to return to Huronia, but, It was to be four years before the missionary could continue his work.

LOUIS HÉBERT COMES TO QUEBEC

"to encourage those who may hereafter desire to inhabit and develop the said country of Canada, the land held by Hébert, is

As we have seen the driving force behind the colony at Quebec was the fur trade. Agriculture, aside from small gardens, was not encouraged and in some cases even frowned on by the merchant traders who harvested the bounty of the forests and streams. Thus, for almost ten years after the founding of Quebec there was virtually no one tilling the soil on a full time basis.

Most of the inhabitants of Quebec were from Normandy and Brittany, but the first true settler in New France was a Parisian named Louis Hébert. Born in Paris in 1575, Hébert was an apothecary with his own shop catering to the elite of French society. One of Hébert's customers was Biencourt de Poutrincourt who enlisted him as a member of his first expedition to Acadia in 1606 where he reestablished Port Royal. It was customary for ships to carry an apothecary to tend the sick, dispensing herbal remedies for the myriad illnesses that plagued the sailors of the day. He was also required to treat any injuries that befell the crew in the course of their duties. Hebert was druggist and doctor all rolled into one.

It is unlikely that Hébert sailed for Acadia with any intention of staying. However, on his arrival at Port Royal he was struck by the beauty of the place and the potential of starting a new life. He decided to settle down in the wilds of Canada. The historian Marc Lescarbot wrote of not only finding Hébert, "sowing corn and planting vines," but, "taking great pleasure in the cultivation of the soil."

When Port Royal was abandoned in 1607 Hébert stayed on and worked his land in peace and happiness for six years, but the lack of support from France and the inherent dangers finally won out. In 1613 he returned to France and reopened his apothecary shop in Paris.

Hébert's life in Paris was a far cry from the freedom and hard work of farming the virgin soil of Acadia. He grew restless and in 1616 he again put up the shutters on his business and joined Champlain for a new life on the St. Lawrence. This time he brought his entire family, his wife Marie Rollet, two daughters and a young son. Hébert was determined to settle in Canada permanently.

The trading company that was backing Champlain promised him a cash bonus, a tract of land and provisions sufficient for their first two years in the colony. In return he agreed to serve without pay as the colony's medical officer, render services to the company as required and most importantly to keep his fingers out of the fur trade. On his shoulders also fell the role of legal officer for the settlement. Not long after his arrival his name appeared on a petition to the king giving his title as *Procureur du Roi*.

Things went badly for Hébert from the beginning. The company only paid him half the bonus and no grant of land was forthcoming. On top of that the company insisted on the bulk of his time for their own purposes. Most men would have packed their bags and headed home, but, Hébert, loyal to Champlain, whom he did not blame for his ill treatment, stayed on. At Champlain's suggestion he began to clear a tract of land above the town without the benefit of title. With the help of some of the townsmen he began to clear twelve acres for planting. It was slow going for he had to do much of the work himself. Stumps had to be burned and pulled, rocks dug up and piled. There were no horses or ploughs in the colony and every inch of the field had to be turned with a spade, a long and labourious task.

Despite setbacks and the work he was required to do for the trading company he had the entire twelve acres cleared and under cultivation within five years of his arrival. Hébert planted a variety of produce on his acreage. Part was sown with maize, part with peas, beans, and other vegetables. An orchard was set off to one side and the balance pasture land. A few cattle were easily provided for in all seasons because of the wild hay that grew on the flats by the river.

Despite the long hours put in for the company and tilling the soil Hébert found time to build his family a fine stone house on his farm. A one story home, it was 20 ft. by 40 ft. and considered one of the most

Townsmen help Louis Hébert clear his land

comfortable in the colony. The hospitality of Madame Hébert and her daughters is found in many of the accounts of life in Quebec in those early years.

It was not until 1623 that Hébert received title to the land he worked. The trading company that controlled Quebec had little interest in agriculture. However, on February 4, 1623 he was granted a large tract of land *en seigneurie* by the Duc de Montmorenci, titular viceroy of New France. In 1626 a further tract on the St. Charles River was granted to him by the succeeding viceroy, Henri de Lévis, Duc de Ventadour. The preamble to this deed read, "Having left his relatives and friends to help establish a colony of Christian people in lands which are deprived of the knowledge of God, not being enlightened by his holy light . . . he has by his painful labours and industry cleared land, fenced them, and erected buildings for himself, his family and his cattle. . . . to encourage those who may hereafter desire to inhabit and develop the said country of Canada, the land held by Hébert, together with an additional square league on the shore of the St. Charles, is given him to have and to hold in fief noble forever, subject to such charges and conditions as might be later imposed by official decree." Thus the French feudal system arrived in New France.

Louis Hébert died in 1627. He left behind a large family who helped the colony grow from a trading centre to an agricultural dynasty in the late 17th and early 18th centuries. Despite his success Quebec was still only a village of sixty-five people at his death, nineteen years after its founding. Louis Hébert was the forerunner of things to come in New France.

CHAMPLAIN LOOKS WEST

"Here is the entrance to the grand river of St. Lawrence."- Champlain on reaching the Bay of Quinte, 1615

Champlain's preoccupation with the establishment of the Quebec colony did not stop him from looking to the west. Aside from his desire to see a permanent French presence in the New World with all that it implied, his main concern was with the fur trade, which, in the short term, was the rational for the whole enterprise. To sustain the settlement a profit had to be realized from the trade in pelts with the Indians.

Champlain cultivated the friendship of the Indian tribes in the Ottawa and St. Lawrence valleys to further these ends. In doing so, as we have seen, it brought the French into conflict with the powerful enemies of the Algonkins and Hurons, the Iroquois. To get the cooperation of his allies in exploring the country Champlain had to aid them in their wars with the Iroquois Confederacy.

Champlain's first penetration to the Great Lakes was August 17, 1615 when he accompanied a large war party of Hurons and Algonkins on a raid into Iroquois territory. It was at the rendezvous at the village of Cahiague that his Huron hosts took him for his first glimpse of the inland sea, the body of water we know as Georgian Bay.

By September 1st most of the warriors had gathered and they set out by way of Lakes Couchiching and Ouantaron (Simcoe) for Iroquois country. They decided to go via Sturgeon Lake, the Otonabi River, Rice Lake and the Trent River to the Bay of Quinte on Lake Ontario. Champlain wrote: "Here is the entrance of the grand river of St. Lawrence."

They crossed Lake Ontario and hid their canoes. They penetrated the woods and crossed the River Chouagen (Oswego), which flows from Lake Oneida where the Iroquois fished. Within seven km of the Onondaga town that was their objective eleven Iroquois fell into the hands of Champlain's men including four women and four children. Iroquet, chief of the Petit Nation, wanted to torture the prisoners, but Champlain strongly objected.

After a period of rest they attacked the village, but instead of following Champlain's plan the Hurons attacked the palisades piecemeal and were decimated by the archery of the defenders. Champlain himself suffered two arrow wounds, one in the leg and one in the knee. The Huron stomach for the fight soon dissipated and the long retreat began.

Champlain suffered from his wounds, writing: "I never found myself in such a hell as during this time, for the pain, which I suffered in consequence of the wound in my knee was nothing in comparison with that which I endured while I was carried, bound and pinioned, on the back of one of the savages."

Champlain wintered with the Hurons at Cahiague on Georgian Bay to recuperate from his wounds. While there he was asked to judge a dispute between the Algonkins of the Petit Nation and the Hurons of de L'Ours. It seems the Hurons had given an Iroquois prisoner to Iroquet instructing him to torture and kill him. Instead of carrying out the wishes of his allies he treated the young Iroquois as a son. On hearing of this the Hurons sent a warrior to murder the young Iroquois and the indigent Algonkins killed the Huron in turn. The two allies were on the verge of war.

The hearings with many witnesses called. After two days Champlain rendered his decision: "You Algonkins, and you Hurons, have always been friends. You have lived like brothers; you take this name in your councils. Your conduct now is unworthy of reasonable men. You are enough occupied in repelling your enemies, who have pursued you, who rout you as often as possible, pursuing you to your villages and taking you prisoners. These enemies, seeing these divisions and wars among you, will be delighted and derive great advantage therefrom. On account of the death of one man you will hazard the lives of ten thousand, and run the risk of being reduced to perpetual slavery. Although in fact one man was of great value, you ought to consider how he has been killed; it was not with deliberate purpose, nor for the sake of inciting a civil war. The Algonkins much regret all that has taken place, and if they had supposed such a thing would have happened, they would have sacrificed this Iroquois for the satisfaction

**Champlain
at
Georgian Bay**

of the Hurons. Forget all, never think of it again, but live good friends as before. In case you should not be pleased with my advice, I request you to come in as large numbers as possible, to our settlement, so that there, in the presence of all the captains of vessels, the friendship might be ratified anew, and measures taken to secure you from your enemies."

During the winter of 1615-16 Champlain was able to make alliances with several tribes including the People of the Petun. Each season Champlain penetrated more and more of the wilderness.

In 1619 Henri de Condé, Viceroy of New France, sold his office to the Duc de Montmorenci and the beginnings of a dispute with the Company of St. Malo and Rouen, which controlled the trade in New France, surfaced. The company sought to discourage settlement and attempted to have Champlain's authority set aside. Finally, in 1621 Montmorenci suppressed the old company and formed the Company of Montmorenci to take over. The agents of the old

company resisted and Champlain was forced to seek refuge in the fort with his armed followers. A Recollet friar was sent to France in an attempt to resolve the dispute. The answer was a temporary merging of the two companies with a number of regulations and conditions, which seemed to have settled the matter.

In 1620 Champlain brought his wife, Hélène Boullé, to Quebec where she was to spend four years. The Indians were struck by her great beauty and she spent her time instructing the women on Christianity.

Things went from bad to worse at Quebec in the summer of 1622. Amid the unrest in the trading community the Iroquois attacked the settlement itself. Fearful of the arquebus they were reluctant to assault the fort, but concentrated on the Recollet monastery instead. The friars had fortified their buildings and were able to withstand the siege. After torturing and burning two Huron prisoners the Iroquois withdrew having disrupted the activities of the entire district in the critical growing season.

In 1624 Champlain returned to France where his wife expressed the desire to become a nun. Champlain refused, but agreed to an informal separation. He sailed for Quebec the following year and never saw Hélène again.

In 1625 the Duc de Montmorenci sold his office to his nephew, Henri de Lévis, Duc de Ventadour. Ventadour's motives for assuming the burden had nothing to do with trade or colonization. He had retired from court and had become a priest; his sole interest was in the missionary activities and the conversion of the Indians. The governance of the colony was left in the hands of Champlain.

Events were fast overtaking Quebec that would temporarily expel the French from Canada.

*

THE END OF A DREAM?

Champlain watched sadly from the taffrail of the *George* as Quebec disappeared from view.-1629

Despite the efforts of Champlain, the colony of Quebec continued to show poor financial results for both the company and the crown. With the ascension of Louis XIII, the son of the great Henry IV, to the throne the prospects in New France became even bleaker. Unlike his father the new king was weak and showed little interest in the affairs of state. Fortunately, the void was filled by the competent and tireless Cardinal Richelieu. He was convinced that the Montmorenci Company was neglecting Quebec and the government would have to get more involved in the affairs of New France. On April 29, 1627, Richelieu came up with his answer: *La Compagnie des Cent Associes*. In the name of the king all other charters and monopolies were voided with the exception of the fisheries and whaling.

The power and influence of the company was to be far reaching. They were granted all the lands between the Arctic Circle and Florida and from Newfoundland to as far west as they were able to explore. The fur trade was to be their exclusive domain for all time. Among the partners was Cardinal Richelieu and many of the important merchants of Paris, Bordeaux and the other great cities of France. Also on the list was Samuel de Champlain, Captain of the King's Marine.

For its part the associates were required to invest three thousand livres each and the company was to adopt the name of La Compagnie de la Nouvelle France. They pledged to bring out three hundred colonists each year and to bring not less than four thousand by the end of fifteen years. They were to support the colonists for three years and supply each community with three priests. All settlers were to be French and Catholic. The government for its part pledged to stand behind the company and supply two warships fully manned and equipped for service. Nothing had been left to chance and on May 3, 1628 the fleet sailed from Dieppe under the command of Admiral Claude de Roquemont and it appeared that a new era of prosperity in the history of New France was about to begin.

In 1621 King Charles I of England granted to one William Alexander all of Acadia, which was called Nova Scotia by the English. This grant included Newfoundland, Cape Breton, Maine, New Brunswick and a large chunk of Quebec. However, aside from a few small settlements around the Bay of Fundy, little came of this grandiose affair. In 1628 war was declared between France and England and the Company of Merchant Adventurers raised a sum of sixty thousand pounds to mount an expedition against the French in Canada. Three ships set out under the command of Captain David Kirke with the duel aim of intercepting the fleet of the Company of One Hundred Associates and driving the French from North America.

Kirke and his two brothers, Lewis and Thomas, sailed into Canadian waters carrying letters of marque. They fell in with de Roquemont in Gaspé Bay where he had taken refuge from a storm in the Gulf of St. Lawrence. The last thing de Roquemont expected was an English fleet in these waters and he was ill prepared to defend his charges. Most of the big guns were stored in the holds of the bigger ships and even the decks of the warships were black with passengers heading for a new life at Quebec. Beside the four ships of the company he had twenty other vessels under his command carrying all the supplies that Quebec would need for the following season.

De Roquemont was a brave and able sailor; the signal "prepare for battle" soon flew from his masthead. The battle was a brief one. Kirke sailed along side the flagship, poured a broadside into her, and boarded. De Roquemont saw the futility of resistance and, to spare the lives of the innocent passenger, struck his colours. The remaining French ships quickly followed suit.

Kirke burned some of the transports and sailed away with the rest as the spoils of war. England hailed the brothers as heroes, while in Paris the three brothers were burned in effigy.

After hearing the news, Champlain paced the ramparts expecting to see the triumphant English banners come sailing up the St. Lawrence. He knew that the colony was doomed, but to his dismay the

Champlain watches his Quebec fade into memory

English sails failed to appear that fall.

Winter came, and without the supplies captured by Kirke the colony was in a bad way indeed. The now fatherless Héberts had prudently stocked their cellar against such a catastrophe, and their generosity kept many a hungry Canadian alive during that long harsh winter. When spring arrived the daily ration had been reduced to seven ounces of pounded peas per person.

Champlain watched from the ramparts for a sign of the relief ships he was sure would come from France. Little did he know that the Company of One Hundred Associates was on the verge of bankruptcy. The relief effort had been bogged down, and when the expected sails appeared, they were English. Captain David Kirke sailed passed the Ile d'Oleans in the *George* and the *Gervase*. Two other ships, the *William* and the *Abigail*, were left at Tadoussac. Kirke sailed in to engage the citadel, but unhappily the men were all in the woods in a desperate search for food. The only man on the ramparts was Champlain. A downcast

Champlain watched as an English officer under a flag of truce walked up the pathway to the fort. The moment that he had dreaded was here, the loss of his beloved Quebec.

Champlain watched sadly from the taffrail of the *George* as Quebec disappeared from view. Kirke graciously allowed Champlain to land at Tadoussac for a last farewell. Now Champlain knew that the English had been guided up river by Frenchmen and inquired as to their identity. The two were pointed out to him and both attempted to escape, but to no avail. Champlain's anger mounted and reached a stormy rage when he discovered that one of the culprits was the long "dead" Étienne Brûlé. Brûlé hung his head in shame and could only offer as a defence the fact that the garrison was doomed and therefore he felt no wrong in helping the English.

Champlain sailed for England and then to France. The English garrisoned Quebec, but the father of New France was not done yet.

The French presence in North America came to an end with the fall of Quebec . Many of the colonists boarded the English ships and sailed back to Europe. Those left at Quebec were Guillaume Hubon and his wife; Marie Rollet, widow of Louis Hébert; Guillaume Hébert; Guillaume Couillard and his wife, Guillemette Hébert and their three children; Abraham Martin, and his wife Marguerite Langlois, and their three children; Pierre Desportes, and his wife Françoise Langlois, and their daughter Hélène; Nicholas Pivert, his wife, Marguerite Lesage, and their niece; Adrien Duchesne and his wife; Jean Foucher; Étienne Brûlé; Nicholas Marsolet, the bailiff; Pierre Reye; and Oliver Le Tardiff.

These French inhabitants who remained were subject to restrictions as to their participation in the fur trade and in the practice of their religion. Catholics were forbidden to pray in public.

Upon landing in England, Champlain immediately began to lobby for the return of Quebec to French control. He pointed out to the French ambassador to London, M. de Chateauneuf, that Quebec had been taken after peace had been concluded between the two countries. Negotiations began and Champlain returned to France to pursue his objective from that end. He sailed from Rye in Sussex and landed at Dieppe where his commission as Governor of New France caught up to him.

He went to Paris where he met with Cardinal Richelieu, the associates of the company and the king. Of course the main topic of conversation was the loss of New France and the means of retrieving it.

Letters were immediately dispatched to King Charles I of England by Louis XIII demanding the return of Quebec and Acadia. The reply from the English king indicated a readiness to restore Quebec, but made no mention of Acadia. The directors of the company immediately ordered a fleet to be made ready under Commander Isaac de Razilly, one of the associates, to take possession of Quebec by force if necessary.

The Company of New France put up sixteen thousand livres for the enterprise and the king underwrote the rest. These preparations raised an alarm in London and Charles I promised to restore the French possessions in America to what they were as of April 24, 1629, the date of the signing of the Treaty of Suze, which ended the conflict.

All this did not sit well with the Kirke brothers who would have preferred a delay so they could profit further from their dealings with the Indians. The English vacillated and the French fumed. The Marquis de Fontenay-Mareuil, Chateauneuf's successor as ambassador received special instructions from Richelieu, "His Majesty's design is that, continuing the negotiations of Chateauneuf, you continue to ask for the restitution of Canada, and all goods and vessels taken from the French since the peace."

The affair dragged on and the English continued to give assurances that Quebec would be restored to France. The French waited and the English stalled. Meanwhile France went to war with Austria, and Canada quietly slipped to the back burner. The negotiations begun in 1629 did not resume until 1632.

These new negotiations proceeded rapidly until the question of the return of goods was broached. The value of the pelts taken from the stores at Quebec were under discussion between Guillaume de Caën and Kirke, and they both disagreed on the sum. De Caën claimed 4,266 beaver skins captured by Kirke while Kirke acknowledged only 1,713 and that the balance of his cargo, 4,000 skins were a result of his own trading with the Indians.

There was skulduggery on both sides. The French claimed all the skins that were in the stores at Quebec at the time of its capture, overlooking those that the English had allowed the French to take with them. Unwilling to get into a fight over something that would be difficult to prove, Charles I ordered the sum of £14,330 paid to de Caën in compensation for his pelts and £6, 060 for the loss of his vessels.

Kirke was furious at this and was determined to seize the pelts taken to London from Quebec, which had been locked up on the orders of a justice. Kirke's associates blew the padlock off the storeroom. When de Caën arrived only 300 beaver and 400 elk skins remained. The king ordered Kirke to restore the skins within three days under pain of imprisonment and the

confiscation of his property.

On March 5, 1632, King Louis XIII received the English ambassadors at Versailles and on the 29th the agreement was signed restoring Quebec and Acadia to French control. The conflict was settled, but darker days were on the horizon.

Champlain made ready to return to his beloved Quebec, and the La Compagnie de la Nouvelle France put together their plans to save the teetering finances of the enterprise. Despite his advanced years Champlain sailed for the New World to repair the damage done during his three year absence.

In Quebec the situation had become intolerable. The English seemed to treat the French well enough, but, the Huguenots among the French were fanatical and Catholic worship was forbidden. Many resolved to leave Quebec at the first opportunity.

On July 13th a vessel slipped into the harbour at Quebec carrying a white flag. Much to the joy of the inhabitants Champlain was seen sitting in the sternsheets of the boat coming inshore. He stepped ashore to the waves and cheers of citizens he had left behind three years previously. All gathered at the home of Madame Hébert to worship, the first mass said at Quebec since the English occupation.

Champlain worked tirelessly to build new houses and improve the lot of the Canadians who worked the land and lived in Quebec. In the fall of 1635 the father of New France became ill and was paralyzed. On Christmas Day 1635 Champlain died, leaving a thriving legacy to the country we now call Canada.

*

At the time that Champlain lay dying in Quebec the directors of La Compagnie de la Nouvelle France were meeting in Paris. One of the items on the agenda was the replacement of Champlain as Governor of New France. No explanation has ever been uncovered as to the reasons why the man who almost single handedly kept the Fleur-de-Lis flying in North

America needed to be replaced. His death made their deliberations prophetic indeed.

The choice of governor fell to Charles Hualt de Montmagny, Knight of the Maltese Order. He landed at Quebec in the summer of 1636 accompanied by his aide, Brehaut L'Isle and a large, distinguished company. There were several gentlemen who had been granted seigneuries, Juchereau des Chatelets, the factor of the company, and some soldiers and settlers, forty-five in all.

Quebec entered a period of prosperity with the arrival of the new governor. The flimsy wooden structures that dominated the town were replaced by stone houses. Private residences began to spring up displacing the barracks-like buildings that housed the predominantly male population. Although the number of people living at Quebec was barely 200 it began to take on the air of a permanent settlement rather than a mere trading post.

De Montmagny enlarged and strengthened the fort and laid out streets around it. A chapel named after Champlain was built behind the fort. A welcome addition to the town was the Hotel Dieu, founded by the Hospitalieres, which was built on the summit overlooking the St. Charles River. Quebec's first hospital was in operation.

Missionaries began to move among the Indians and many were converted to Christianity. Into this fertile mission field came the first devout French women who were to make their mark in Canada history.

Marie de l'Incarnation, a widow, entered the Ursuline convent in Tours in 1633 leaving the care of her eleven year old son to her family. In April of 1639 she set sail from Dieppe for Quebec where she landed on the 31st of July. The nuns were welcomed by de Montmagny where a dinner was given in their honour and a bonfire lit to celebrate the birthday of the Dauphin. The next day they were taken by boat to Sillery where they were to build their monastery.

Duties were set out with Marie de l'Incarnation as superior, Cecile de Saint-Croix as apothecary and cook and Marie de Saint-Joseph as the teacher of the Indian girls left in their care.
Le Jeune, the Jesuit, began teaching the nuns the Algonkin and Montagnais languages. They soon became proficient in these as well as Huron. The future looked bright for nuns and Indians alike.

Within a few weeks de l'Incarnation met her first Huron, a Christian named Joseph Chihwatenha, who had accompanied the traders from Georgian Bay. He spoke little French but communicated his admiration for the Ursulines with his eyes. The visit was to be a turning point in the history of the Huron Nation.

No sooner had Joseph and the Huron traders left for home when disaster struck. Smallpox, brought on the ships from France, flared up at Quebec. This was bad enough among the French, who had some resistance to the disease, but for the Indians the plague was catastrophic. The Indian immune system had never seen smallpox and the disease spread through the villages like a wildfire. By November a full fledged epidemic was ravaging the Indian population. Those at the monastery were not immuned and the house was full of the sick and dying.

The nuns worked tirelessly to nurse their charges. They were forced to lay mattress on the floor so tightly that it was difficult to move among them. A temporary hospital was also crowded with dying and terror strickened Indians. The Ursulines used up all the bed and body linen they had brought from France, a supply that was to have lasted two years. Even their headbands were used as bandages. Four of the girls died by the time the disease had run its course in February 1640.

In the villages the carnage was horrible. No lodge was spared and the sick were too weak to bury their dead. Some blamed Christianity for their troubles imagining a spiritual demon had been loosed among them. Others rightly blamed the French for their afflictions.

In Huronia the traders who had been to Quebec carried the plague back with them and the once powerful Huron Nation was felled, not by the Iroquois war club, but by the diseases brought by Europeans. Whole villages were wiped out that summer and winter. The balance of power in the region was altered forever. The Iroquois would seize the opportunity to reek havoc on their enemies.

THE MARTYRDOM OF ISAAC JOGUES

"On the way, they were beaten with such fury that Jogues, who was last in the line, fell powerless, drenched in blood, and half dead. As chief among the French captives, he fared the worst. His hands were mangled and fire applied to his body."

With the return of Quebec to French control the Jesuit missions reopened and Huronia welcomed the priests with open arms. As we have seen, the results were disastrous as smallpox swept the villages one by one. Despite this the missionaries began to have some success in converting the Indians to Christianity. The Jesuits continually looked south where the Iroquois held sway while toiling among the Hurons, Algonkins, and their allies. They knew it was their duty to evangelize them in spite of the dangers involved.

The opportunity came in 1642. Father Isaac Jogues had been among the Hurons, Petuns and Algonkins since 1636 and was considered one of the best missionaries in the field. He had once preached to two thousand people at the rendezvous at Sault Ste. Marie. In the summer of 1642 he was chosen to take much needed supplies to the Huron missions, a dangerous assignment as a great number of Iroquois were known to be raiding in the St. Lawrence Valley.

Jogues set out in August with a party of thirty-six Hurons and three Frenchmen in twelve canoes. The French contingent consisted of René Goupil who, having some medical experience, was going to Ste. Marie as surgeon; Guillaume Couture, a man of great devotion and courage; and a labourer. The canoes were threading their way through the islands at the west end of Lac St. Pierre where the heavily wooded slopes were hidden by tall reeds. Suddenly, out of the reeds, sprang a number of canoes filled with Iroquois warriors. Caught off guard, the battle was short. Three Hurons were killed and twenty-two taken prisoner along with the Jogues and his French companions. After plundering the canoes the raiders headed south up the Richelieu with their prisoners.

At every stop along the way Jogues and his companions were tortured before marching on. Finally they reached Mohawk country where they were paraded through the three chief villages. They were ridiculed, beaten with clubs, their fingers broken or cut off and their bodies burned with red hot coals. Couture had slain a Mohawk warrior during the brief battle on Lac St. Pierre, but he held up so well to the

torments inflicted on him that one of his captors adopted him to replace a dead relative and he escaped further torture. Goupil, after several months, was killed. Jogues, despite his suffering, survived, glorying in the opportunity to preach the gospel to his tormentors.

After several months he was taken to the Dutch settlement at Fort Orange (Albany) with a fishing and trading party. The Dutch had been lobbying the Mohawks unsuccessfully for his release after hearing of his capture from another trading party. They took full advantage of his presence among them and, braving the wrath of the Mohawks, helped him escape.

Jogues found passage on a Dutch ship and reached France where he was greeted as a saint and martyr snatched from the jaws of death. According to the laws of the church he could no longer administer the sacraments with his mutilated hands, but the wilds of Canada called him and, with a special dispensation from Pope Eugenius IV, he headed once more for the rigors of the Canadian wilderness.

The next missionary to reach the Iroquois was an Italian Jesuit named Father Joseph Bressani. On April 27, 1644 he set out with six Hurons and a twelve year old French boy from Trois Rivières. It was thought that the Iroquois had not yet penetrated into the valley this early in the year, but the party was ambushed by twenty-seven Mohawks who killed several of the Hurons and carried the rest along with Bressani and the boy to the Mohawk villages.

Bressani was tortured even more severely than was Jogues and only survived because an old Mohawk woman adopted him. The boy was not spared and stood up to the test until death relieved him of his suffering. Bressani's hands were so badly mangled that his value as a slave was minimal. The Mohawks took him to Fort Orange to be sold. The Dutch gave a generous ransom; and gave Bressani passage on a Dutch vessel, which landed him at La Rochelle on November 15, 1644. Like Jogues, his one thought was to return to Canada and in the following year he was

Isaac Jogues in the hands of the Iroquois

in Huronia, his torn and broken hands mute witness to his courage.

Missions among the Iroquois seemed to be a forlorn dream until an incident in 1645 opened the door. A band of Algonkins captured several Mohawks and brought them to Sillery to be dealt with in the customary fashion. The captives were fully resigned to the fate that surely awaited them, torture and death. However, the Jesuits at Quebec and the governor, Montmagny, persuaded the Algonkins to free the prisoners, then treated them with kindness. They sent one off to initiate peace talks. Guillaume Couture, by this time a trusted member of the community, advised the Mohawks to send ambassadors to Trois Rivières to consult with Montmagny. The talks produced a temporary peace and the Mohawks agreed to bury the hatchet.

In the spring of 1646 Montmagny decided to send a special envoy to make the peace permanent and establish a mission among them. Isaac Jogues was

stationed at Ville Marie at that time and his knowledge of the Mohawk language and his character made him the logical choice for such a mission. Memories of his suffering was still very fresh in his mind and he shrank from the task, but just for a moment. He set out and on his arrival at the Mohawk villages he found a friendly welcome. The Mohawks listened to the governor's message and accepted the wampum belts and gifts, which he brought as a sign of good will. At last both Jogues and Couture felt that the time was ripe for an Iroquois mission; *the Mission of the Martyrs.*

On leaving the Mohawks he left a locked box as a pledge of his return and by the end of June he was back in Quebec to report on the success of his journey.

At the end of August he set out, along with a lay brother named Lalande and several Hurons, to redeem his pledge. Jogues had a premonition of death. On the eve of his departure he wrote a friend in France: *Ibo et non redibo,* I shall go and shall not return.

On his arrival at the Richelieu some Indians told him of a change in the attitude of the Mohawks. They were in arms and threatening vengeance against the French and their allies. The Hurons abandoned them, but, Jogues and Lalande pushed on into Iroquois country where a band of Mohawks seized them on the trail, tied them and led them into the Mohawk villages. They were stripped of their clothes and were beaten and tortured as before.

The cause of this change was the locked box left by Jogues as his pledge. The drought and sickness that visited the area was attributed to the box. Despite his protests the torturing continued. Finally on October 18, as he lay battered and starving in a hut, a chief came and invited him to a feast. Jogues knew that this was a feast of death, but he followed the chief. As he bent to enter the longhouse a warrior positioned by the door buried a hatchet in his skull. The following day Lalande suffered the same fate. Their heads were cut off and mounted on the village palisade and their bodies were thrown into the Mohawk River. The *Mission of the Martyrs* was at an end.

THE BIRTH OF MONTRÉAL

I have not come here to deliberate, but to act. It is my duty and my honour to found a colony at Montréal; and I would go, if every tree were an Iroquois! De Maisonneuve to Montmagny 1641

The slow growth of New France was a sticky subject at the court at Versailles. The Company of One Hundred Associates became the convenient scapegoat for the problem. When the company's charter ran out in 1663 the English colonies to the south boasted a population of one hundred thousand and the Dutch colony on the Hudson River a further ten thousand. New France's population stood at a mere three thousand. Despite its early troubles the company actually met its commitments underwriting a steady flow of settlers to Quebec.

The pressure to expand the colony grew, and in 1641 the company commissioned Paul de Chomedey de Maisonneuve to found a settlement at Montréal. A woman, who was to figure prominently in the history of Montréal, was also included in the group.

Jeanne Mance was born in 1606 into a family of the lesser nobility. Her father held the post of King's procurator. She had read the *Jesuit Relations*, the account of the missions in Canada, and swept by an intense spiritual conviction, was determined to go to New France and work in the missions. She went to Paris to pursue her dream even being granted an audience with the Queen. Women in high places flocked to hear her expound her ideas, but it was to be a woman of lesser birth that was to galvanize Jeanne into action. Madame de Bouillon, widow of the Superintendent of National Finances, became very interested in Jeanne's work. Her husband had left her a wealthy woman and after much deliberation she agreed to fund the founding of a hospital in Canada.

Jeanne set out for La Rochelle and a ship that would take her to fulfill her destiny. On the way she heard of a special mission, the founding of Montréal, and she knew her course.

Three ships set sail from La Rochelle. The ship carrying Jeanne Mance was the first to arrive having been separated from the others enroute. Jeanne was surprised at the less than enthusiastic reception her party received. It seems that the governor, de Montmagny, was not consulted on the establishment of the new colony and had let his disapproval be known to the population. De Montmagny felt that the new Montréal enterprise was an infringement on his prerogatives as governor.

De Maisonneuve's ship finally limped into Quebec on August 20th. The tension became obvious from the first meeting of the leader of the Montréal expedition and the governor. Miffed at the lack of consultation, the governor tried to dissuade de Maisonneuve from going up river. The Iroquois were raiding all along the river and the island would be hard to defend. He offered him Ile d'Orleans to settle his people, but de Maisonneuve was determined to press on. The governor was at least able to persuade him to wait until spring to go to Montréal.

The winter was spent preparing for the move. De Maisonneuve supervised the construction of boats to transport the needed supplies. A three masted pinnace, two half-decked shallops, a barge, and a boat for navigating the shallows were constructed.

With the coming of spring the expedition got under way. The governor and several prominent citizens of Quebec accompanied de Maisonneuve and his party. De Montmagny was the first to see the Island of Montreal in the early evening dusk. They had sailed from Quebec on May 8 and had taken nine days to reach their destination. They had not seen or heard a single Iroquois warrior on their journey.

The next morning they landed at Pointe a Callières and as de Maisonneuve came ashore he fell to his knees and all followed suit. A prayer was said and a hymn of thanksgiving sung. The officers donned their finest uniforms and the priests their vestments for Mass. The women of the party had raised an altar and, with the soldiers on guard with loaded muskets, the small party worshipped.

After the Mass, the Jesuit, Father Vimont, said, "That which you see is only a grain of mustard seed. But it is cast by hands so pious and so animated by faith and religion that it must be that God has great

Jean Mance and the first hospital in Montréal

designs for it. He makes use of such instruments for His work. I doubt not that this little grain may produce a great tree, that it will make wonderful progress someday, that it will multiply itself and stretch out on every side." Prophetic indeed.

The next day a palisade was constructed for the defence of the new colony and the governor formally handed over control of the Island of Montréal to de Maisonneuve. He then boarded his ship and sailed for Quebec.

All that summer the boats plied the river bringing supplies from Quebec. Despite the expectations of an attack, nothing was seen of the Iroquois that summer, although there was little doubt that they watched the progress of the settlement. By the time fifteen soldiers arrived in September houses and a chapel to accommodate sixty people was in place behind the stout palisade. On the feast of the Epiphany, January 6, 1643, de Maisonneuve had a path cleared through the snow to the top of Mount Royal where a large

cross was erected as a symbol of the faith of those that had traveled across the sea to this wilderness called Canada. Jeanne Mance established her hospital and served the little community without respite. Ville Marie de Montréal was born.

*

The small settlement of Ville Marie de Montréal thrived in its initial year. The Iroquois left the new colony in peace through that critical first winter and all seemed quiet. With the coming of the second winter the settlers relaxed as the season of the Iroquois was passed. Their complacency was short lived. Even though the winter was harsh, with snow falling constantly, the Mohawks began harassing the little settlement, picking off anyone who dared venture out into the countryside.

At this stage of the colony's life it was blessed with an alarm system second to none, a faithful female dog named Pilote who patrolled the surrounding woods. Whenever she picked up the scent of the Iroquois she would raise the alarm making a surprise attack on the fort next to impossible. After giving birth to a litter of puppies she taught them to follow her example. The mother and her brood patrolled constantly giving ample warning of the presence of hostile Indians in the neighbourhood.

With the approach of spring the soldiers grew tired of their forced confinement in the fort and persuaded de Maisonneuve to allow them to sally forth against the enemy. De Maisonneuve reluctantly accepted their proposal.

On March 13th Pilote gave the alarm and de Maisonneuve led thirty well armed men forth to teach the Iroquois a lesson. The instant they entered the woods de Maisonneuve knew he had fallen into a trap. Arrows whistled through the woods and the angry bark of muskets told him that the Iroquois had a great number of guns at their disposal.

The French took cover but, it soon became apparent that they were outnumbered and the Indians were outflanking their position. By his own estimates de Maisonneuve figured that his thirty men were facing at least a hundred Iroquois. The order to retreat was given and a mad dash was made for the hospital along a path that had been cleared to haul logs up to it. Iroquois burst from the woods in hot pursuit, oblivious to the guns of the French.

To the watchers at the fort it seemed impossible for the soldiers to make the safety of the hospital before being overtaken. In desperation they fired over the heads of their comrades with little hope of hitting anything at that range. Whether this slowed the enemy or the French were fleet of foot we will never know, but they made shelter with nothing to spare. De Maisonneuve himself was nearly captured while covering his men's retreat. Three Frenchmen were killed and a number wounded. Jeanne Mance had her first patients. The Iroquois remained in the vicinity for the balance of the winter.

PISKIART, WARRIOR PRINCE

"He is one of those people who bear on their foreheads something, I know not what, worthy of empire, and to see him with a bow or a sword in his hand one would say that he is an animated portrait of those ancient Caesars of whom we see in Europe only copies all blurred with smoke." Father B. Vimont describing an Algonkin warrior, Jesuit Relations, Vol 26

Despite their successes against the French the Iroquois did not have it all their own way. The Hurons fought well when confronted and the Algonkins, a brave and fierce race, had driven the Mohawks from the St. Lawrence Valley after Cartier's visit. To the Algonkins also belonged the privilege of producing the greatest warrior of the day. His name was Piskiart.

Piskiart lived in the Ottawa Valley and became a Christian at an early age. Perhaps it was to get the musket that the French sometimes entrusted to converts. Whatever his reason, he became a devout Christian in his old age. He was tall with a handsome, intelligent face and he could move through the woods with the stealth of a cougar. Unlike his brothers who, Piskiart preferred to fight as a lone wolf. He more than proved his worthiness to be called the greatest

warrior of his time when he went alone into enemy country, a one man war party.

On reaching a village he found a convenient woodpile on the edge of the forest and made a hiding place under it. After dark he stole into the village and killed every man, women and child in one lodge without disturbing either his victims or the rest of the village. From his hiding place the next morning he could hear the weeping and the shouts of rage. Warriors searched only to return empty handed.

The second night, thinking the killer would not dare return, the village bedded down for the night. Piskiart repeated his attack, slaughtering the occupants of another lodge quietly slipping back to his hiding place. Again the warriors vainly searched for

Piskiart sets a Deadly pace in fleeing the Iroquois

this phantom intruder while the wails of grief poured from the distraught village. When he emerged from his hiding place on the third night he found a string of sentries surrounding the village. Killing one of them, he raised a wild war whoop and departed with the Iroquois in close pursuit. This time he made no effort to conceal himself, but headed for home on a clear path. All through the day the chase went on, the pursuers taking turns setting the pace to run their quarry to ground. However, Piskiart did not tire, keeping a steady pace throughout the day. The Mohawk warriors finally gave up the chase and set up camp for the night, exhausted after the long, grueling run. As they lay sleeping Piskiart slipped back and killed the entire party with his tomahawk.

The Iroquois decided that they needed time to recuperate from a war that had not gone very well and using as a pretext two warriors spared by the Algonkins at the behest of Montmagny, they agreed to talk peace. In July 1645 a delegation arrived at Trois Rivières led by a chief named Kiotsaton. The Iroquois were known for their great orators and Kiotsaton was no exception. Addressing Montmagny by the name given him by the Mohawks he began his speech, "Onontio (Great Mountain), give ear, I am the mouth of all my nation. When you listen to me, you listen to all the Iroquois. There is no evil in my heart. My song is a song of peace." He handed over seventeen collars of wampum each symbolizing a term of the treaty.

When all had been settled Piskiart, chosen to give Kiotsaton a gift of furs, stepped forward wearing new buckskin leggings and moccasins, which were richly decorated with beads. He eyed the Iroquois chief and said, "O Kiotsaton, consider these gifts as a tombstone that I place above the graves of those who died in our last meeting. May their bones be no longer disturbed. May revenge be thought of no longer."

The short lived peace with the Five Nations had begun.

THE DESTRUCTION OF THE HURONS

"Two days after their defeat the news came to us that all the warriors were killed or captured. It was toward midnight it was announced to us and at once in all the cabins were weeping, tears, and pitiful cries." Fr. Joseph Chaumonot, 1649

The uncertain peace between the French and their allies and the Iroquois lasted but a short time. Whether the pact was a ruse to allow the Iroquois to gather their strength or they had genuinely wanted peace we will never know. By the summer of 1646 war parties again began to waylay the trading canoes on their way to Quebec. The Algonkins and their allies in the St. Lawrence and Ottawa Valleys, weakened by disease, were no match for the warriors of the Five Nations. Many Algonkins fled to the safety of Quebec or to the Hurons on Georgian Bay.

Except for the destruction of Contarea, a Huron stronghold four miles from present day Orillia, in 1642 the Iroquois had done little but send small raiding parties into Huronia. Under this relative tranquility the missions flourished with the main post at Ste. Marie and satellite villages scattered throughout the country including St. Louis and St. Ignace.

The Jesuits were finally winning converts and by 1648 their were twelve mission stations. The Hurons were even helping by working among the Petuns in the Blue Mountains south of Nottawasaga Bay and the Neutrals living between the Grand River and Niagara. The missionaries were looking farther afield toward the unexplored regions around Lake Superior to expand their efforts to Christianize a continent. Their hopes were soon dashed as the victorious Iroquois finally turned their fury on Huronia.

There was no communication with Quebec in 1647 because of the Iroquois presence. In 1648 Father Bressani took an escort of 250 Huron warriors to go to Quebec to replenish the dwindling supplies of the missions. As soon as they started their descent of the Ottawa an Iroquois war party, which had wintered on Lake Nipissing, moved toward Huronia.

The Huron town that marked the southeastern boundary of Huronia was St. Joseph or Teanaostaiae with a population of 2,000. Father Antoine Daniel was the missionary in charge and had just returned from a retreat in Ste. Marie. On the 4th of July he was celebrating Mass in the chapel, which was crowded with people. No sooner had he finished than the dreaded cry of "Iroquois, Iroquois!" rang through the town. When he rushed outside Father Daniel could see that the Iroquois were already hacking through the palisades and the defenders were falling before the onslaught of musket balls and arrows. His frightened congregation huddled in the chapel and when he stood in the doorway and faced the warriors he was struck down in a hail of arrows. His body was thrown into the burning chapel and after slaughtering many of the inhabitants they put the whole town to the torch. A small village nearby suffered the same fate and when they were done they marched back to their own country with over 700 prisoners.

The Grand Council of the Confederacy of the Five Nations now decided on the complete destruction of the Huron Nation. A war party of 1,200 warriors spent the winter of 1648-49 on the upper Ottawa River. Although the Hurons were apprehensive they felt that they had time yet to prepare for the inevitable confrontation with their ancient enemy. While the ice remained in the rivers no raid was possible.

As the first colours of dawn streaked the sky on the 16th of March, the Hurons sleeping peacefully in the town of St. Ignace awoke to the dreaded Iroquois war whoops. Before they could recover, the Mohawk and Seneca warriors had breached the walls and the slaughter began. Three Hurons managed to escape and rushed to warn St. Louis of the pending danger. The women, children and those to ill to fight were sent on their way to Ste. Marie. The Hurons begged Father Jean Brébeuf and Father Gabriel Lalemant to flee to Ste. Marie, but they refused insisting that in the hour of danger their place was with their flock.

There remained at St. Louis about eighty warriors and they were determined to defend the town. The Iroquois, having made short work of St. Ignace, descended on St. Louis where the Huron warriors made a valiant stand. Outnumbered ten to one, the outcome was never in doubt. The victors soon broke the defence and captured all those remaining alive including Brébeuf and Lalemant. What followed was

The Iroquois massacre Hurons at St. Ignace

one of the most savage pages in Canadian history.

The two priests were bound and led back to St. Ignace where a special platform was erected so that all could witness the torture of these two black robes. Brébeuf, big and strong was the first to be led to the stake. After stripping him of his clothes he was tied to the stake which he kissed before his torment began. He called out encouragement to his companions. They began by scorching his body with torches and pulling out his finger nails. In a diabolical reference to baptism they then poured boiling water over his head. Despite this Brébeuf uttered no cry of pain. One of the most common tortures used was the collar and this was applied to the tall priest. A wreath of green wood was hung with six hatchets heated white hot and put around the neck. When the victim leaned forward to rid his chest of the excruciating pain, the hatchets would sear into his back. To the disappointment of the Iroquois Brébeuf made no cry nor did he move. They wrapped him in a bark belt smeared with pitch and set it on fire, Yet he still did not cry out, but exhorted his

tormentors and begged forgiveness for them. After four hours his heart was torn from his body and consumed by the warriors as was the custom when a prisoner died bravely. The frail Father Gabriel Lalemant survived eleven hours at the stake before death relieved him of his suffering.

Survivors of St. Ignace reached Ste. Marie with the horrible tale of the martyrdom of Brebeuf and Lalemant. A rescue party of 300 from Nottawasaga rushed to assist, taking a short cut passed the tip of Lake Isaragui (Mud Lake) and these were able to drive the first Iroquois they met before them. However, they soon faced the entire war party and they in turn were surrounded and after an all day battle all but thirty were killed. This probably saved Ste. Marie from the same fate as St. Ignace and St. Louis.

When the Iroquois departed the missionaries went to St. Ignace and recovered the broken bodies of their confreres. Among the witnesses was Christophe Regnaut, the boot maker of Ste. Marie. He wrote,

"We buried these precious relics on Sunday, the twenty-first day of March, 1649, with much consolation . . . When we left the country of the Hurons, we raised both bodies out of the ground and set them to boil in strong lye. All the bones were well scraped, and the care of drying them was given to me. I put them every day into a little oven which we had made of clay, after having heated it slightly; and, when in a state to be packed, they were separately enveloped in silk stuff. Then they were put into two small chests, and we brought them to Quebec, where they are held in great veneration."

The Huron Nation was dispersed all over the country. Ste. Marie was burned by the French and its inhabitants fled to St. Joseph Island near Michilimackinac. Some Hurons sought refuge with the Neutrals because of the ancient right of sanctuary in their land. Still others fled further west to be absorbed into the many tribes that lived in the country around and beyond Superior.

The Iroquois reigned supreme and the settlers of the St. Lawrence quaked in fear of warriors of the longhouse.

INDEX